Essential Ethics:
A Buddhist Approach to Modern Day Life and Social Action

other books by
Geshe Dakpa Topgyal

Death A Natural Part of Life

Diamond Key for Opening the Wisdom Eye:
A Guide to the Process of Meditation

Holistic Health: A Tibetan Monk's View

The Quest to Safeguard Wholesome Family Life

Refuge

The Tibetan Buddhist Home Altar

Two Subtle Realities: Impermanence and Emptiness

Your Mind, Your Universe

Zuflucht — Buddhistische Zufluchtnahme

Essential Ethics:
A Buddhist Approach to Modern Day Life and Social Action

Geshe Dakpa Topgyal

Radiant Mind Press
CHARLESTON, SOUTH CAROLINA

Copyright © 2007–2022 by Geshe Dakpa Topgyal

Photo credits / permissions: Sunset Ashoka pillar at Kutagarasala (front cover), Rufous, Adobe Stock; Snow lions, Barry Barnes, Adobe Stock; Chapter ornament, Азиза Сейфутдинова, Adobe Stock; Lotus sketch, designer_an, Adobe Stock; Geshe Topgyal, Dakpa Topgyal personal photograph.

All rights reserved. No part of this book may be reproduced in any form or by any means, electronic or mechanical, including photography, recording, or by any information storage and retrieval system or technologies now known or later developed, without permission in writing from the publisher. For permission requests, write to the publisher at the address below.

Print ISBN 978-1-952518-07-2
ebook ISBN 978-1-952518-08-9

Published by Radiant Mind Press
12 Parkwood Avenue
Charleston, South Carolina 29403
radiantmindpress@gmail.com

Acknowledgments

THIS BOOK WOULD NOT have been possible without extraordinary support from a number of people. I have to begin with thanking my students Sara Graham, Grace Rice, Cheryl Novak Condy, Kristin Hess, and my friend Kathy Crowe for their generous support and tireless work on correcting the originally published manuscript over several times.

Several good Dharma friends encouraged me to write a book on essential ethics that could be applicable to normal everyday life in our normal society. I thank them too.

I also want to thank my lovely niece Passang Chokey for helping me type the initial manuscript.

For the 2022 reprint of *Essential Ethics*, minor revisions were made throughout to clarify meaning and add more headings. Otherwise, the content replicates the 2007 version. I thank Sheila Low-Beer who retyped the book after the original manuscript could not be located, proofed the reproduced manuscript, and consulted in the production process. Cynthia Laurrell formatted the book, also proofed it, and shepherded it through republication.

Finally, I pray and hope that this book on ethics by a simple Tibetan Buddhist monk will help people ethically heal—from their home to the universe.

Homage

The practice of ethics can be relied on to lead
to the perfect path to the state of liberation.

Ethics is the supreme and core essence
of the Buddha's doctrine.

It is declared as Pratimoksha, the root of the
attainment of individual liberation from Samsara.

I pay heartfelt homage and prostrate to Buddha,
the all-knowing one.

Author's Dedication

May the merit from writing this book

bring peace and happiness in all existing realms.

May His Holiness the Dalai Lama have a long life.

*As a result of virtue
I shall dwell in the spacious,
fragrant and cool heart
of a lotus flower*

~ Shantideva

Contents

INTRODUCTION 1

Chapter 1   Ethics: The Indispensable Basis for All Good Qualities and Spiritual Realizations   5

Chapter 2   The Ethics of Ten Virtuous Deeds   13

Chapter 3   Abstaining From Actions That Cause Negative Social Consequences   29

Chapter 4   Ethical Standards for the Media   39

Chapter 5   Ethical Conduct of Parents Is a Vital Factor in a Child's Upbringing   43

Chapter 6   The Principles of Moral Conduct in Society   47

Chapter 7   Becoming Good Human Beings Through Training in Moral Conduct   57

Chapter 8   Formal Ethics of Pratimoksha   61

Chapter 9	The Source of Immoral Conduct: Negative Thoughts and Emotions	75
Chapter 10	Benefits of Individual Liberation Ethics	79
Chapter 11	The Ethics of a Bodhisattva	83
Chapter 12	The Four Ways of Magnetizing Living Beings Towards the Dharma	97
Chapter 13	The Commitments of Training in Bodhicitta	101
Chapter 14	The Ethics of Tantra	109
CONCLUSION		113
Appendix A	The Life of Buddha and His Fundamental Teachings	117
Appendix B	Kayas	133

Introduction

MANY PEOPLE THINK OF ethics and morality as merely religious concepts. They think that a serious consideration of ethics is reserved for seriously religious people.

I think that this attitude is mistaken.

This book is written to help readers understand the importance of ethics and to find a way of establishing basic ethical and moral principles regardless of religion.

Ethics is the foundation and the beginning point of Buddhism, and as a monk, I write from the Buddhist perspective. But these insights are applicable to anyone, religious or not. They are universal ethical guidelines for all worldly interactions and for individual spiritual development.

Our world is facing a glut of ethical crises at every level—from the family to the international level and even to outer space. Ethical principles are sometimes lacking in every important field—education, medicine, politics, business, science, arts and environment. World peace, prosperity, security and harmony can only spring from the cultivation of ethical and moral conduct. Ethical conduct must begin with the individual and then extend outward to influence the larger world.

This book emphasizes the individual's responsibility for his or her own actions. Establishing good karma and merit through wholesome conduct and helping others is the most direct route to improving the condition of the world as well as the best method for gaining personal happiness. These benefits are powerful incentives for ethical conduct. Although supplication and prayers are better than nothing, they cannot compare with the power of heartfelt ethical actions.

The historical Buddha Shakyamuni taught that ethical conduct is the foundation for spiritual development and for the growth of basic human goodness. Lord Buddha persistently emphasized the importance of moral conduct for peace and harmony from the family to the universal level. In his final words before departing into *parinirvana* (the dissolution of his physical appearance from the eyes of the ordinary world) he said:

> *There is no need to appoint anyone as my successor. Rather, you should treat my teachings on moral and ethical conduct as your unerring teacher.*

So you can see the paramount importance and usefulness of moral conduct for our spiritual development, of living our lives with a commitment to non-violence and inner self-discipline.

Becoming a spiritual person is not as important as becoming an ethical person. Many of the emotional conflicts that are experienced by people all over the world can be resolved by establishing inner discipline through the cultivation of morality. Moral guidelines and ethical behavior are essential for living a meaningful life and for the well-being of others. For those who accept the Buddhist view of karma and rebirth, morality can be valued for its beneficial effects on future lives.

I have written this book on ethics with the hope of being helpful to people who are serious about bringing these concepts into their daily lives. Therefore, I sincerely request that all readers practice ethical conduct as much as they can. The practice of ethics is all about internalizing rightness, wholesomeness, truthfulness, sincerity, honesty, humility and compassionate concern for others without being preoccupied with self-centeredness.

To be a good and ethical person is the best way to make positive contributions to our human world. Living with proper moral guidelines is what distinguishes human beings from all other living creatures.

Ethics is not just a religious concept. It is something that is essential for the growth of all that is good and constructive.

With prayers,

Geshe Dakpa Topgyal
March 2007

Ethics: The Indispensable Basis for All Good Qualities and Spiritual Realizations

BUDDHISTS, LIKE DOCTORS, BELIEVE the first rule of ethics is *Do no harm*. The second rule is *Do all you can to help others around yourself.* These are values everyone shares.

Buddha taught that good ethics is the foundation for spiritual practice, so Buddhists have examined ethics in great detail. There are many specific practices that encourage ethical behavior, even different schools of ethics. All Buddhist approaches emphasize the importance of motivation and working in harmony with natural law.

Ethics is not, however, a religious concept. Ethics is a human concept. People naturally want to reduce human suffering and increase peace, happiness and harmony. Ethics is the basis for the peace, happiness and harmony that we all seek. Most of human suffering stems from unethical and immoral actions and thoughts motivated by greed, lust, hatred, ignorance and self importance.

Ethics is like a fertile soil where all seeds can grow and bear fruit. The farmer makes sure that the soil contains necessary nutrients, and that it is free of rubble, weeds and poisonous plants. Similarly, pure ethical discipline nurtures higher spiritual training, including meditation and insight into the true nature of reality.

Proper cultivation of ethics helps you eliminate actions and thought patterns that are enormous barriers to your spiritual growth. Pure ethics also nurtures positive qualities. So if you neglect ethics, then you really do not know how to practice Dharma. Dharma is a Sanskrit word that literally means teaching or path. For a Buddhist, following Dharma means following the path laid out by Buddha. For non Buddhists it means following your own spiritual path.

To be ethical is the most important part of Dharma practice. There is not much meaning to any other spiritual practice if you are not an ethical person.

What Is the Buddhist Concept of Ethics?

For Buddhists, ethics means voluntary self-discipline, refraining from actions that cause pain and suffering in others or yourself. It also means doing your best to help others, or, if that is not possible, at least doing no harm. This fundamental commitment to doing no harm, or *ahimsa*, is motivated by concern for others and is central to ethics in Buddhism. Buddhists believe that good results come from good motivations, and bad results from bad motivations.

To cultivate ethics, you need to understand how your actions and thought patterns make a difference in your own happiness, and the happiness of others. This is a unique potential of the human mind, heart and brain. And so it is extremely important to investigate the connection between what you do and how it affects other people. If an action would help you but cause others to suffer, you must not do it.

Ethical discipline and compassion must go together, hand in hand. One without the other does not have much meaning and cannot lead to any higher purpose. Compassion is the strong feeling of the unbearableness of others' suffering, along with a clear recognition of suffering and pain. Compassion will not distance you from others nor will it overwhelm you with sadness and hopelessness.

Ethics must be cultivated in all fields—social, religious, educational, medical, scientific, political, etc. Otherwise, any human endeavor can lead to pain, suffering and even environmental and global catastrophe. Unethical and immoral actions always eventually create unexpected problems, confusion and psychological illness. Just because something is possible through scientific means does not mean that it should necessarily be pursued. We must clearly understand the ultimate outcome.

For example, development of unlimited atomic and chemical power has changed our world in amazing ways. But we must be careful this knowledge does not violate natural law or make our world a dangerous place where people live in constant fear. Unfortunately, it is clear the world today is more vulnerable and dangerous as a result of scientific and technological development, with serious threats of nuclear, chemical and biological weapons.

In the medical field, we need to look at areas like stem cell research, cloning, and keeping a dying person on an artificial life support machine when there is no hope.

Stem cell research can bring disaster if done for commercial gain or the mere fulfillment of scientific fantasy and ego, which would be unethical and immoral. On the other hand, stem cell research can lead to an understanding of how some diseases develop, and eventually lead to cures for conditions like Parkinson's disease. Stem cell research may one day even lead to the replacement of body parts.

Human cloning is unnecessary and unethical from every point of view. It is meaningless and a human disaster. Cloning a human baby will not make better human beings on earth nor will it improve living conditions. The only justification for cloning would be cloning a perfectly enlightened person!

The only proper motivation for scientific involvement in human reproduction must be genuine compassion. Any other motive will lead to abuse and exploitation. The ability to manipulate the sex of a baby is really an impressive achievement, but it can violate the natural law of cause and effect (karma), or what other religions call God's will. Even if you do not believe in karma or God's will, still there is a violation of the law of nature. Furthermore, manipulating the sex of a baby can cause psychological confusion and create deep emotional suffering.

At the other end of the life cycle, keeping a dying person on artificial life support machines when there is no hope of living a meaningful life violates and disrupts the natural process of death. Artificially extending life affects the patient's consciousness, which may very well feel suffocated and painfully stuck in an artificial body, which is no longer of any benefit to him or her. Such suffering cannot be ethical.

In short, science and technology can bring great achievements and benefits, but they must not violate the laws of nature and the laws of cause and effect (karma). In the Buddhist view, that inevitably leads to disaster. Natural law is harmonious, creating the physical world, its structure and all the living beings who enjoy the natural world. Altering natural processes creates disharmony and imbalance and the effects are eventually always negative. As an old commercial put it, *It's not nice to fool Mother Nature!*

Only when science embraces moral principles, ethics and karma can it truly reduce suffering and bring happiness for humanity. Science and spirituality should work together. They are both meant to improve the quality of life and the living environment, creating causes and conditions that lead to happiness and dispelling causes and conditions that lead to suffering and pain.

I would suggest that the wisdom backed by the compassion for all creatures should be the fundamental moral ground for both science and spirituality. Then scientific knowledge and spiritual wisdom will be used solely for finding the best tools for peace, happiness and security for all creatures, as well as the best way to protect our planet.

This will prevent irreparable negative consequences that can go beyond our control.

There are also moral dilemmas in matters of life and death, law and faith, science and spirituality, legal punishment and useful legal correction, etc. I will address some of these conflicting arguments in detail in later chapters.

The central point is that for Buddhists, ethics means voluntary self-discipline, refraining from actions that bring pain and suffering, and compassionately helping others and ourselves.

Three Levels of Buddhist Ethics

The voluntary commitment to avoid causing harm is central to the three levels of ethics in Buddhism. These three levels are increasingly subtle and demanding and each one incorporates the previous one. A person may choose to take a vow to follow any of these levels depending on his or her individual motivations and spiritual goals.

Pratimoksha

Pratimoksha is a Sanskrit word which means liberation from painful *Samsara* (endless rounds of birth, death and rebirth). These endless rounds, caused by karma and our own tendencies, are ultimately the result of ignorance of the true nature of reality. This level of ethics centers on refraining from all deeds of body, speech and mind that cause harm. The proper practice of Pratimoksha disciplines your body, speech and mind, which provides the foundation for the Bodhisattva and Vajrayana ethical training.

Bodhisattva

A Bodhisattva is a high spiritual being who, out of compassion holds back from entering Nirvana to remain and work to relieve the suffering of all living creatures, without exception. This level of ethics of compassionate concern is called *the vows of a Bodhisattva*. The main practice is striving to restrain from selfishness, cultivating the cherishing of others and devoting oneself to helping others.

Vajrayana

On this level, the practitioner strives to see everything as pure divine emanation, worthy of the highest enjoyment. Vajrayana practice is appropriate only for people who have a great deal of spiritual maturity.

The Vajrayana vows are higher than the Bodhisattva vows. The Bodhisattva vows are higher than the Pratimoksha vows. However, one cannot take the Vajrayana vows without first taking and perfectly keeping the Bodhisattva vows. One cannot take the Bodhisattva vows without first taking and perfectly keeping the Pratimoksha vows. Therefore, it is extremely important to take and perfectly keep the Pratimoksha vows.

~~~

The first two levels of ethics will be the main subject of this book. The Pratimoksha and Bodhisattva precepts reflect the teachings Buddha gave to help all people find relief from the suffering nature of samsaric existence and to gain the everlasting peace of Enlightenment. The Vajrayana teachings were reserved for those who had already gained significant spiritual maturity and realizations.

The short chapter on tantric ethics included in this book simply introduces the reader to this advanced stage of ethical conduct. It would be counterproductive to address the topic in detail here since it is necessary to first master the preliminary precepts.

The Ethics of Ten Virtuous Deeds

NO SANE PERSON WAKES up and says, *Today I'm going to be immoral and unethical*. We all try to do the right thing, and some of us work hard on our spiritual growth. Yet we're still human, and our needs and wants and delusions get in the way of our noble goals.

The only way to overcome these obstacles is by watching our thoughts and motives—with vigilance, patience and also some kindness towards ourselves—and then striving to do better. We also need to understand that whether we are motivated simply by the desire to avoid bad karma, or by heartfelt loving kindness, it is not always easy to make the right choice. It takes discipline, self respect, a deep sense of consideration for others, and conscientiousness.

And, as we shall see, many ethical dilemmas are very complex, and it's not always easy to figure out the best solution.

At the most basic level, we want to refrain from causing harm (even against our own self interest), but we also want to actively help others. This can range from simply wishing that others were free from suffering, to being committed to helping whenever possible, to being willing to sacrifice everything, including our bodies, to free others from suffering.

The Buddhist ethical code falls into two categories: informal and formal. Informal ethical conduct centers on a wholesome way of living, avoiding ten classes of negative actions, but without any formal vows. Formal ethical vows, which can be taken by laypeople, monks and nuns, will be discussed in a later chapter.

Buddhists divide the ten kinds of negative actions into three groups: physical, verbal and mental.

Negative physical actions:

1. Killing
2. Stealing
3. Sexual misconduct

Negative verbal actions:

4. Lying
5. Slander
6. Harsh or abusive speech
7. Senseless talk or idle gossip

Negative mental actions:

8. Covetousness

9. Harmful intent or ill will

10. Wrong views or rejection of truth

These ten negative actions are similar to the ten commandments of the Jewish and Christian faiths, but are seen as more a matter of natural law than religious doctrine.

In Buddhism, motivation largely determines the spiritual impact of the action, although this is not true in every case.

In general, if we are motivated by greed, lust, anger, hatred, pride, malicious intent or harmful ideas like racism, then the action is negative regardless of how it might seem on the surface. Similarly, when we are motivated by love, compassion, kindness or selflessness, then the action is naturally positive, even if it seems bad on the surface.

So you can't judge whether a person is acting in a positive or negative way without clearly understanding their motivation.

It's obviously extremely important to examine your own motivation closely. Whatever you do should not cause suffering, and your own gain should not mean someone else's loss. A mindful compassionate concern for others is crucial when you are deciding whether to do something for your own personal gain.

It is foolish to lose sight of long term negative consequences for the sake of short term gain. The pleasure of a sweet taste of honey is nothing compared to the pain of cutting your delicate tongue when you lick honey on the hidden razor blade of selfishness. And the pain of the consequences will last a lot longer than the momentary pleasure of temporary gain.

The Three Negative Physical Actions

Killing

Killing means taking the life of any conscious creature, including one that has natural potential to become a life. It also means shortening a lifespan, either directly or indirectly. This includes abortion, mercy killing, euthanasia, capital punishment and destroying a fertilized egg, either frozen or in a woman's uterus.

The act of killing becomes complete in the moment that a person feels a sense of satisfaction or relief upon the death of the victim.

This seems straightforward, but even here, the situation can be complex. In the case of frozen embryos, for instance, if the motivation for killing the embryo is scientific research to find a cure for disease, then the action isn't necessarily negative.

In general, abortion is a serious crime by the natural law of karma. It means killing an innocent life who has done nothing wrong to anyone, and who is under your compassionate care, affection and protection. The mother provides the baby's safe and protected home. The baby places all his or her trust and hope in its mother.

Its mother's face is the first thing that a child can recognize right after birth, with no need for introduction. So if you kill that innocent child it is a heartless crime and against human nature.

However, there can be a few exceptions to this view. If a pregnancy would kill the mother, then termination may be the correct moral decision for the parents to make. Or if the fetus is so badly deformed its life would be one of much suffering for both the child and the parents, that too can justify abortion. However, the action is still not one hundred percent positive and ethical from the karmic point of view.

Another complicated situation, to take an extreme example, would be if killing one person would spare many other innocent people. If the motivation was compassion for the killer and for the victims, killing could be then justified.

Capital punishment, on the other hand, is absolutely wrong and negative. It serves no purpose for either the one being killed or the executioners. Killing in the name of legal punishment is a serious mistake in human law.

Capital punishment is nothing other than hateful revenge, deriving pleasure from the other person's death.

Killing someone in the name of legal punishment only kills the physical body. There is no way to kill a soul or mind. The soul or mind only continues in a different body in another life, carrying the same tendency toward crime, eventually coming back into society. In a real sense, the problem remains the same.

Therefore, instead of imposing a death sentence, we should help people correct their thinking and behavior, and then bring them back to normal society, in this life or the next, without their being a threat.

Then prisons would truly be *correctional institutes*.

Most killing is motivated by lust, jealously, greed, envy, malicious intent, extreme ideologies of racism and religious bias, confusion or fear. These acts are not just criminal from a legal standpoint; they are serious crimes against natural law.

Killing a human being is the most serious of all. Killing your mother, father or a high spiritual being is considered a crime with immediate retribution, with boundless negative consequences through the natural law of karma, where action is inevitably followed by reaction.

Killing for food, clothing, self-protection, or for economic purposes is less negative. Still, the motivation is really attachment to existence, as well as attachment to mere comfort in many cases.

The best diet, accordingly, is vegetarian. If that is not possible, the best approach is not to become too attached to eating meat. For instance, don't spend the day anticipating that steak you're having for dinner. If you can't have meat, don't be disappointed. In general, it is extremely important to refrain from killing all conscious creatures and to cultivate a deep sense of respect for their right and freedom to live on this planet. Their lives are as precious as your own life. They have the same right and freedom to live.

Stealing

Stealing simply means taking something you know is not yours, no matter what its value or quality. It can mean stealing in quick, sneaky ways, or by force, bullying, threatening, trickery or borrowing with no intent of returning. Stealing includes using military force to gain control of oil or other economic resources in another country.

Stealing food, clothing and medicine for survival are considered less negative. Stealing out of greed, desire, jealousy, hatred, resentment, and for comfort are all very negative and unethical acts. Stealing religious objects, church and temple property, public property, and anything that is dedicated to higher charitable and spiritual purposes is considered extremely negative and criminal.

A more subtle act of stealing is borrowing money (or any object) from someone and deliberately failing to pay it back. Maybe you wait and watch to see whether your friend has forgotten about the loan. When you realize he or she has forgotten the matter, then suddenly you feel you don't have to pay it back. In that very moment you have fully committed the negative action of stealing, because stealing is considered complete in the instant you feel that the stolen object is now yours and no longer your victim's.

If you find an unclaimed object in the street, it is best to give it to a charitable organization, a temple, or other public use.

The mindful refraining from stealing is a direct way to give material prosperity to others and the karmic cause for you to be wealthy in a future life.

You should not seek comfort and luxury at the expense of others. Luxurious living is inappropriate and immoral in any case, and especially when someone else pays the price. Many politicians and government officials travel on first class tickets and stay in five star hotels at the expense of hardworking taxpayers. I feel strongly that this is very inappropriate and unethical. It is nothing other than misusing public money and property for one's own comfort, luxury and enjoyment. This misuse of public property, by the laws of nature, has a heavy karmic consequence.

Sexual Misconduct

Sexual misconduct includes having sex with someone else's husband or wife, or with someone who is in a committed relationship or engaged to be married, or against the will of the other person, which of course includes rape.

The act is made fully complete when the two sexual organs meet.

Generally sexual misconduct is motivated by lust (extreme attachment to sex), but it can also be motivated by hatred, such as a man sleeping with the wife of an enemy.

It is also sometimes done out of ignorance, such as thinking that through sexual intercourse one can gain spiritual realization. Sexual intercourse is part of natural life. However, sexual intercourse which is full of fantasies and distorted excitement can in no way help a person gain spiritual realization.

Sexual misconduct is negative and it creates much pain and suffering. It is clear that faithlessness causes many broken marriages. Children from broken marriages are the first victims of their parents' sexual misconduct. Children of divorced parents often seem less happy than children of intact families. They experience more failure in school and get into trouble more often. Also, they are often deprived of the opportunity to develop positive and ethical behavioral characteristics due to the lack of good role models. When children of divorce grow up, they may be more likely to think that divorce is a normal part of married life. It is extremely important to know that as a parent one has full responsibility to teach your children through setting a good example, and to bring them into human society with good moral conduct.

It should be noted, however, that divorce by itself is not necessarily unethical. Sometimes it is the kindest thing for the parents and for the children. But divorce is negative when it is the result of someone's own selfish interest, ignoring the interests of innocent children.

Sexual misconduct can also cause unwanted pregnancies, which can lead to abortion, a negative act of killing an innocent life which has the right to be welcomed into the world. Most abortions are due to simply not wanting to have a fatherless child, or the embarrassment of an out-of-wedlock child, or being financially unable to raise the child. In these cases it is clear that taking an innocent life is motivated solely by self-interest. This abortion is caused by the mindless and irresponsible sexual activity, which falls into the category of sexual misconduct. (As noted above, abortion to save the mother's life does not fall into the same category.)

It is extremely important to know that sexual misconduct has so many negative consequences. It directly affects a wide range of people, impacting their emotions, friendships, relationships, as well as social prosperity and harmony.

In Western cultures, overemphasis on sex and the glut of sexual images are the primary causes for sexual misconduct and the suffering it causes. Explicit sexual images and information are available on television, in magazines, movies and the internet. This is very harmful for children.

It is extremely important to do something about this collectively and to work on improving the moral values of family and married life. Sex with no moral boundaries is negative and it threatens the values that lead to harmonious and happy human lives.

Sexual misconduct is a misuse of the natural potential of sex to be a meaningful, enjoyable and beneficial part of a committed relationship between adults. Sex is an expression of pure love, commitment and sharing. It is also a compassionate act of reproduction, to nurture the spiritual and physical well-being of offspring while passing on the genetic traits of the parents.

Love is a pure understanding of who the other person is. It is not based on any physical characteristics or any other superficial attributes of the other person. Lust, as opposed to the normal human urge for sex, is an unhealthy sexual feeling looking only for self-gratification and temporary relief from burning sexual desire.

Love should be based on true committed love instead of lust and sexual fantasy.

The Four Negative Actions of Speech

Lying

Lying means deliberately telling an untruth to lure or deceive others. An act of lying is complete the moment the other person understands the message of your words or gestures. The other person does not necessarily have to believe you.

The main intention of lying is to confuse the other person, whether through speaking, or nodding the head, or gesturing with the hands or eyes. Any action done with the deliberate intention to confuse someone constitutes lying.

Lying about one's spiritual attainments and higher psychic powers, such as clairvoyance, is considered to be particularly serious. It is like feeding poison to another person. Many of the present day cult leaders' words to their followers fall into the category of spiritual lies, and it can really ruin the lives of their followers. It is extremely important for both the spiritual teacher and the follower to be aware that this type of lying is seriously negative, harmful and dangerous.

In general, there is no reason to talk about one's spiritual realizations even if one has experienced higher realizations. The student should not be too concerned about the spiritual teacher's realizations. Instead, they watch what he or she teaches and if the teacher follows the teaching in his or her own life. This is the healthy and safe way to follow one's spiritual teacher.

Divisive Talk/Slander

Divisive talk or slander means intentionally causing dissension between family members, friends or people in a spiritual community. Divisive talk is complete in the moment another person hears the divisive talk, whether it causes division or not.

In general, you should not talk mindlessly when part of a social gathering. Think about why you are at the gathering and what you should talk about and what should be avoided. Mindful conversation on relevant issues, conducted with a helpful motivation, is extremely important and necessary for human interaction. This surely helps prevent many unnecessary problems, confusion and disharmony.

If someone speaks divisively, you must decide whether to ignore it, leave, correct the comment, or make a positive comment to counteract the negative one. If you speak up, others will see you as a decent person and treat you with respect and trust.

Verbal Abuse/Harsh Speech

Verbal abuse/harsh speech means intentionally using unpleasant words, trying to cause emotional pain. Verbal abuse includes insulting, humiliating and defaming speech, as well as pointing out another person's faults and imperfections, whether true or not. The negative action of verbal abuse is complete the moment the abusive words are heard by the person to whom they are directed.

Idle Chattering/ Senseless Gossip

Idle chattering/senseless gossip means chattering without any reason or just talking mindlessly. Gossip often includes pointing out someone else's faults and mistakes or covering up your own mistakes and wrongdoings. It can also include fantasies about unpractical and impossible things, or arguing just for the sake of argument.

Idle gossip is negative because it creates delusions and wastes the precious energy of everyone in the group.

The Three Negative Actions of Mind

Covetousness

Covetousness means desiring other people's possessions for yourself. An act of covetousness is complete the moment you generate a strong attachment to someone else's possessions and wish they were yours. Coveting can be directed at material belongings, relationships or personal qualities. Attachment, jealousy and wanting to separate someone else from his or her possessions are the main factors of covetousness.

Harmful Intent/Ill will

Harmful intent/ill will means wanting to hurt someone with or without a reason. This includes the hope that others will suffer misfortune and fail in their activities. The negative act of ill will is completed either when the harm is inflicted or the mental intent is completed.

Ill will has five components:

1. A basic motive of hatred, anger or lack of tolerance
2. Lack of realization of the destructiveness of anger
3. Intention to do harm
4. Lack of enough realization of danger of the harmful intent to overcome the harmful intention

5. Holding on to the wish that another person will suffer harm

One should cultivate love and compassion towards others as an inner antidote to harmful intention.

Wrong View/Denial of the Truth of Reality

Wrong views, or denial of the truth of reality, means a blind rejection of what truly exists. You might reject the existence of something out of ignorance, because you have not seen it or believed it in the past. When you reject the existence of something that actually does exist because of your blind and biased attitude, then the negative action of wrong view is fully completed.

In general, there are four types of wrong views in the spiritual realm: wrong views about cause, about effect, about function, and with respect to the interrelatedness of all things.

A wrong view about cause means not believing in karma. A wrong view about effect means not believing that intentional actions in the present do affect outcomes in the future. A wrong view about function means believing that causes do not produce effects, and that there is no past life or life after death. A wrong view about the interrelatedness of all things means believing that anything can exist by itself without being part of the universe, which would make Enlightenment and Nirvana impossible.

Not believing in the connectedness of all things and in the law of karma are said to be the worst wrong views, and the root of all imperfections and flaws.

You should not believe anything out of blind faith and bias, but instead seek to find truths that do not contradict valid reasoning and valid perception. However, it is not right to dismiss something just because you haven't seen, heard or experienced it. You would have to be omniscient to verify every single thing that exists! But it is possible for ordinary people to develop the purity of mind and the analytic skill to ascertain correct spiritual views. This will help you overcome delusions and the suffering they cause.

~~~

For happiness, peace, prosperity and harmony, from the individual to the global level, you must make a conscious effort to refrain from the ten negative actions of body, speech and mind which create suffering in the present and in the future. This is not easy. It requires cultivation of inner discipline, self correction and self control, vigilantly keeping an eye on your mind and its impulses.

To help refrain from the ten negative actions, it is extremely useful to begin every day with a renewal of virtuous affirmations. When you first awaken in the morning, your mind is in a calm and gentle state and not yet involved with any worldly thoughts. Here is one set of meaningful affirmations to begin your day:

~ *Oh, precious life! I must use it in a meaningful way.*

~ *I will abstain from killing any form of living being, including the smallest insect.*

~ *I will abstain from taking what is not mine.*

~ *I will abstain from wrong sexual activity.*

~ *I will abstain from telling lies, using insulting speech, slandering others, and indulging in gossip or senseless talk.*

- *I will abstain from drugs, alcohol, and other abusive substances which dull and alter the mind and destroy the sense of judgment that allows me to distinguish between what should be cultivated and what should be discarded.*

- *I will respect the right of others to be happy.*

- *I will be humble, sincere and honest in every action of my body, speech and mind.*

- *I will check on my own shortcomings before pointing the finger of blame at someone else.*

- *I will help others if the help is within my means and capability.*

Abstaining From Actions That Cause Negative Social Consequences

Over-Consumption

GIVEN THE RAPID DEPLETION and the inequitable distribution of the world's resources, consumption is an ethical question that concerns everyone.

We should not consume more than we need for our survival and modest comfort. Excessive consumption of things like food, clothes, water, construction materials, gasoline, electrical power, and so forth is generally motivated by the desire for entertainment, ostentation and greed. This is wrong and morally very negative.

Our over-consumption will create suffering for our future generations. Our own grandchildren will become the first victims of the mindless and greedy over-consumption of this generation.

Over-consumption destroys our global natural resources and pollutes the environment, creating many unexpected illnesses and other elemental disasters, such as global warming. Many of the world's big companies go to third world countries, undeveloped countries or poor countries to cut down their trees for lumber, drill for oil, mine their earth and construct polluting industries. The companies make a lot of money and leave behind a polluted and ravaged land. The people who live there suffer while the big companies grow richer.

Large international companies must have ethical concern, wisdom, moral responsibility and long-sightedness as part of their mission. Natural resources are not meant to be a source of profit and exploitation for a small portion of the world's population.

To be ethical means to protect yourself and others from unexpected pain and suffering. Every educational, economic, scientific, medical, political, artistic and business endeavor must have proper strict moral guidelines. Working to satisfy selfish interests causes moral corruption. Big companies who violate and ignore the well-being of others and undertake immoral work for their own immediate economic gain will eventually collapse from the problems that are the inevitable results of this moral corruption. Shortsighted efforts to maximize profits not only harm living creatures and the environment, they eventually harm the corporations themselves.

On a personal level, our consumption of material goods must be governed by a sense of concern and responsibility for the earth's dwindling supply of natural resources. We must be aware of what is required for survival and basic comfort—what is necessary, and what is not necessary. When we make purchases, we need to try to send that money where it will do more good than harm, and try to support companies that are sensitive to the environment and to the happiness of their workers.

What we eat must be food and not bait. Food is what we need to sustain our fragile physical body. Bait is just for sensory pleasure, comfort, and satisfaction of desire—and it doesn't do the fish any good. Bait can be harmful to your mind, body and wallet. Ethicists and nutritionists would agree on the health benefits of a simple, unrefined diet. Similarly, whatever you wear should represent your unique culture and serve the real purpose of protecting the body from the elements.

In this modern electronic world, we over consume for ease, comfort, pleasure, and temporary enjoyment of our life. None of these serve the real purposes of life. Consider how we use gasoline. We drive huge SUVs, vans and trucks to transport one person from here to there. We use big boats, jet skis, and many other vehicles just for fun and pleasure.

Clearly, over-consumption driven by desire and greed is immoral and unethical. We should all be very mindful about our daily consumption, with a compassionate concern for the well-being of future generations and for the physical environment that sustains us.

Destruction of the Natural Environment

As human beings, each of us has an ethical and moral responsibility to protect the natural world. All living beings have an equal right to live in a healthy environment. Our superior intelligence is not meant to be used to destroy the natural environment.

Toxic chemical pollution or taking out minerals and other natural products from the earth and water create natural disasters and immense mental and physical health problems. We all have an equal responsibility to take care of our natural environment.

Wrong Livelihood

A wrong livelihood means making a living that does harm, while many different, positive means of making a living are available. Examples of wrong livelihood are selling, making, distributing and giving weapons, poison, alcohol, tobacco, drugs and other abusive and addictive substances. Running a brothel, prostitution, gambling, and operating a factory that produces toxic waste are all wrong means of livelihood.

Fishing, operating a meat company or chicken farm, or raising animals for slaughter are also considered wrong livelihoods because it is preferable to be a vegetarian. However, most people do eat meat. In that case, it is important to consider the way animals are raised. Some animals have a happy, healthy life. But some animals suffer and live in filth their whole lives and this is a terrible thing. We should consciously choose the food we eat wherever possible. We should buy organic vegetables and grains that have been raised without polluting the earth with chemicals, and if we eat meat, choose free range or organic meat where the animals have been well cared for and not given antibiotics and hormones that hurt the animals, hurt the people who eat the animals, and hurt the environment.

Making a living through flattery, hinting, intentionally seeking reward for favors, pretentious behavior, and contriving are the *five wrong means of livelihood* to be refrained from, particularly by ordained monks and nuns.

You should not adopt these types of wrong means of livelihood while many other right means of livelihood are available in your world.

Racial, Religious and Ethnic Discrimination

Racial, religious or ethnic discrimination is very negative and endangers world peace, harmony and understanding. We must be aware of these qualities in ourselves and make a moral effort to refrain from bias and discrimination at all times.

Many of the world's problems and conflicts are rooted in racial, religious and ethnic discrimination and hatred, like the social problems and conflicts in Somalia, Bosnia, China, Africa, Nigeria, Russia, Yugoslavia, Sri Lanka and other parts of the world. We must focus on the high value of all human beings rather than on race, color, religion and ethnic origin. Superficial differences are unimportant when compared with the real value and meaning of human life. Racial, religious and ethnic discrimination brings nothing positive to the individual level or to the planet, but instead brings disharmony, conflict, war, killing, control, hateful suppression and oppression, fear, anger and hatred that are transmitted from generation to generation.

The only way to bring peace and harmony in the world is through destroying discrimination and hatred and replacing them with tolerance and respect. Each of us must cultivate love and compassion and a genuine understanding of the value and meaning of human life.

A Three Step Exercise to Cultivate Tolerance and Respect

Visualize three people standing in front of you. One is your enemy, the second is a loved one and the third is a stranger. With an open mind, look at them from their own point of view. You will come to see that all three have the equal right to be happy and free from suffering. This insight will help overcome the tendency to be biased. You will see every one is equal in that way.

Once you have a pretty good understanding of that, the next step is to see all as dear to your heart. From that feeling of closeness comes the automatic sense of concern and desire for them to be happy. That feeling of closeness and genuine concern is called love.

Compassion is the third step. It is the pure understanding of the right of all to be happy and your moral responsibility is to help them as much as possible, if that help is within your means and ability.

Every human life is precious and sacred, with an equal right to live and share the world. All human beings are basically the same, with blood that is red regardless of race, religion or ethnic background. There is more reason for brotherhood and sisterhood than there is for considering one another strangers or enemies. There is more ground for cultivation of love and compassion than for racial and ethnic hatred and discrimination.

An ethic of refraining from racial, religious and ethnic bias and discrimination is essential for global peace, harmony and stability. A political or religious leader must not encourage hatred and discrimination toward other people for their own political and religious interest, power or control.

Disregarding Truth and Justice

This involves taking into account the grievances of both sides of a conflict in a manner that is based on truth and justice. Many of the world's problems that lead to so much killing and suffering are due to the inability on the part of some governing body to resolve the conflict in a fair and unbiased manner. For example, the unresolved conflict and political problems between the Palestinians and the Israelis are due to the biased and one sided approach on the part of the problem solvers.

We must act in accordance with truth, justice and impartiality in every issue from the individual to the international level. This is the only way to resolve global conflicts and disharmony, and to build reliable mutual trust and friendship.

Disregarding truth and justice is very negative and unethical conduct. We must be respectful of the value of truth and justice and live with the understanding that they are essential to harmonious relationships at every level.

Acknowledging and Taking Responsibility for Our Wrongdoing

Sincerely acknowledging our wrongdoing and taking full responsibility is extremely important and very useful in resolving conflict and disharmony. A sincere and truthful acknowledgment of our wrongdoing helps us to correct our actions, cultivates respect for the feelings of others and enhances our own dignity.

A sincere and truthful acknowledgment does not mean humiliation or embarrassment. Rather, it is a part of being honest and respectful. From a religious point of view, it is extremely important to go through spiritual correction of body, speech and mind.

Sincerity, honesty, humility, taking responsibility and being respectful should be part of our character. These qualities will not come to you from outside. They must be internally cultivated through seeing their positive benefit and moral value. Refusing to acknowledge your wrongdoing is negative and unethical by nature. It is the same as being untruthful and inconsiderate to others' feelings and views. Being truthful, accepting responsibility and trying to rectify misdeeds is the same as being sincere, honest, just and respectful.

Failing to Help Others When You Are Able to Do So

Choosing not to help others when you can is immoral and unethical conduct. This is surely not human nature. Always choosing to help others, regardless of who the other person is and how she or he relates to you, is a unique feature of human moral conduct. You must not hesitate to help others if you can. The help should be given without making any biased judgment on the worthiness of the person in need of help.

Giving sincere help to others is the most precious gift you can make. By nature, help is its own reward. The giver of help is rewarded as well as the receiver. Developing the habit of giving help is beneficial to the one in need, to the general quality of life, and it is also of huge benefit to your personal happiness.

Abstaining From Actions That Cause Negative Social Consequences

Short-term Pleasures with Long-term Negative Consequences

Many of the long lasting negative consequences of misdeeds come from the desire for short term pleasure and benefit. You must not do anything for personal interest and benefit that has longterm or short term negative effects for others. It is important to carefully examine what you do with a mindful and compassionate concern for others' well-being. There are four things to consider before making a decision to do anything for personal gain:

1. No action should be taken if there are negative consequences for others, even if there is benefit for you.
2. An action should be taken if there is positive benefit for others, even if there is temporary loss for you.
3. Nothing should be used for your own enjoyment at the expense of others.
4. No action should be taken if there are longterm negative consequences, even if there are short term benefits and gain.

Ethics is all about doing things in a wholesome way with a right motivation and a mindful concern for the outcome of our actions. Mindfulness is a remedy for all harmful activities that come from selfishness and shortsightedness.

Be mindful in every activity of your daily life and in all interactions with the world around you.

Ethical Standards for the Media

NEWSPAPERS, TELEVISION, MOVIES, VIDEO games and magazines should not emphasize sex, violence and lurid behavior, which are extremely bad for the society in general and for children in particular.

One of the reasons why the various media place their emphasis on sex and violence is that this is an easy way to make money. Many viewers enjoy the sensations provoked by this sort of material. Producing such unwholesome entertainment is an example of promoting self interest at the expense of the wider community.

Media Responsibilities

The various branches of the media have a huge potential to influence the world in both positive and negative ways. Therefore, media have a responsibility to place more focus on positive and ethical aspects of human nature. Good news is not remarked on precisely because there is so much of it. Bad news is repeated over and over on television, newspaper, radio, magazine and internet with much exaggeration and in some cases with many lies. The media should report what is actually going on instead of reporting what they think should be reported. This is why most people in the world are deeply confused by the political lies from politicians and governments.

The media should be unbiased, honest and precise. The media should not manipulate the news for their own interest or the interest of their friends.

What is to Be Reported as News?

The saying goes that when a dog bites a person, that is not news because that is normal and happens all the time. When a person bites a dog, that is unusual, and so it is newsworthy. Just so, the media must know what is news and what is not news before reporting to the world.

Killing innocent women and children in the name of war is news and it should be precisely reported to the world. Killing a soldier in the war battlefield is not news because it is meant to be. Carrying a gun to fight someone who is also carrying a gun is the job of a soldier. Killing someone who does not have a gun, like innocent women and children in their own home, is not the job of a soldier. It is important to introduce the principles of ethics even as a part of military training.

Television, movies and magazines should aim not just to make money, but also to spread useful information on health, science, religion, history, medicine, arts and other humanitarian, beneficial topics.

Ethical Conduct of Parents Is a Vital Factor in a Child's Upbringing

THE ETHICAL CONDUCT OF parents is a most precious gift for their children. There is no imaginable material gift that can equal the gift of moral values, which can help your child live a life that is happy, compassionate and content. This inner contentment is true wealth, a precious jewel that makes it possible to have a life that is calm, peaceful and fully happy with what is available.

When compassionate caring and moral values are absent from a home, and when the child is morally neglected by the parents, it is clear to see the damaging effects. The child tends to feel insecure and selfish and the mind is often agitated and aggressive. Conversely, when a child receives good, loving guidance in a morality based home, the child tends to be much happier, less selfish, more secure and more confident. It is easy to see when a child comes from a morally sound home, with loving parents who are concerned not only for themselves, but for others as well.

A morality based loving environment at home is extremely important because children can easily learn negative behavior and selfishness from their parents. The parents are the first and most important teachers in their children's life. If, for example, the father and mother are always arguing, or frequently lying to one another, the child may at first find this objectionable, but gradually comes to see this behavior as quite normal. The child will then take this learned behavior out of the home into the world. As a result, he or she will become very unhappy and destructive.

As a parent, you should not smoke, drink, argue, lie, kill, steal or use harsh words in front of children. You should teach about real moral meaning and value. It is vital to teach your child the importance of basic human good qualities and moral values such as honesty, sincerity, humility, love, compassion, non-violence and respect for the rights of others. It is very wrong to emphasize the importance of money, selfishness and self importance.

For instance, parents should not make money the most important factor of a child's life. Instead, parents must understand that warmhearted and ethical conduct is the most important factor of a child's life. Parents must not allow children to watch all types of mind corruptive television images and violent movies. I have noticed that some parents deliberately allow their children to watch television in order to have personal time to chitchat with their relatives and friends. Television and movies serve as babysitters in the Western world. This has the potential to be ethically damaging for the children.

Home discipline is extremely important. It is the parents' responsibility to provide proper moral discipline for their kids.

Parents must understand that moral discipline is the root of all goodness and it provides a healthy psychological environment for the growth of learning capabilities at school. Many of the children who have learning problems and get into trouble at school come from homes that lack moral discipline and a healthy atmosphere. Unfortunately, when the child fails at school, the parent and society often blame the teacher. This is morally very wrong and irresponsible.

The teacher's job is to teach, motivated by compassion. The parents' job is to discipline their kids at home within a wholesome environment. The parents must know that the school is the source of education and knowledge. Home is the source of discipline and rules of ethical conduct. It seems to me that most of a teacher's time at school is consumed by disciplining the students. There is not much time left to teach. The parents' first job is to teach the children how to develop ethical discipline and a compassionate heart, and the rest largely depends on the children themselves and the teachers.

The rules of ethical discipline are not just rules set by the parents for use at home. They will serve the child as a universal guide to a wholesome discipline that naturally facilitates the growth of all that is good, wholesome and beneficial. They will give the child confidence in his or her own ability to deal with life. Self confidence is a critical factor in a child's ability to learn.

To be a good parent is not easy at all. To be a good parent means rearing children with an ethical discipline, sense of responsibility and compassion by serving as role models of proper behavior. Parents must know how to teach ethics to their kids through action as opposed to through words. In all matters of ethics, discipline is only really effective and useful when it comes from within.

The Principles of Moral Conduct in Society

THERE ARE SEVERAL PRINCIPLES of moral conduct that must be cultivated by every human being regardless of religious belief and cultural tradition.

Religious belief and cultural tradition have nothing to do with the cultivation of principles of moral conduct that are required for harmonious relations, from the home to the international level. These principles are the basis for happiness, peace, harmony and for the growth of genuine feelings of intimacy among fellow human beings. They are covered in this chapter.

Honoring Your Parents

It is extremely important to know that parents are the kindest beings on the earth because they are the ones who gave us selfless love, protection, care and nurturing in our lives. Our parents are our first teachers, who guide us in the right direction with moral values and education. Parents are the source of lifelong merit and virtue.

We could not survive in life without our parents' love, care and protection. Even when we have grown up and become independent we must not forget the kindness of our parents. Forgetting the kindness of parents is surely not normal human behavior, and is a real sign of the degeneration of moral values in human society.

Even if you have been abused as a child you can still work towards healing those emotional and psychological wounds and coming to forgive your parents.

The degeneration of moral values and ethical behavior towards parents is in many ways a major cause for failing in life. To be close to your parents and to honor them is not just an Eastern value. It is a basic human moral duty, and must be cultivated by every one of us. Such moral conduct seems to receive less emphasis in cultures with excessive materialism. The lack of love and respect between parents and children seems to be a major cause for dysfunctional family relationships.

Therefore, it is important to improve the quality of parent/child relationships by focusing on basic moral values. Parents must provide genuine love, affection and caring for their children. Children must not forget the kindness of their parents and respectfully honor their parents at all times. Children must cultivate humility, obedience, respect and a sense of closeness towards the parents. Also, the children must take full moral responsibility to serve their parents when they need help and support.

Honoring the Learned Ones

Honoring and respecting members of society who are particularly learned and wise has many benefits for the individual as well as for society as a whole. The men and women who exemplify the highest values can serve as models and teachers for the rest of society. It is important to pay special interest to their wisdom and to have an openness to learn from them. They should hold the most honored positions in society because they show the way for truly solving the world's problems. The more attention we give to their wisdom and knowledge, the more we will be in a position to gain understanding and goodness from them.

Even on an individual level, you can honor your kind teachers, those who have helped you or who have changed your life.

Therefore, it is important to place special value on the learned and knowledgeable ones, and make an effort to obtain their knowledge and wisdom for oneself.

Honoring and Respecting Elders

Honoring and respecting elders in our society is the moral duty of younger people. It is immoral and negative to disregard, insult and alienate elders just because of their reduced ability to perform normal functions in the conventional world. Younger people must take full moral responsibility for paying attention to and looking after the needs and wishes of the elderly. Unfortunately, in the

West, old people are sometimes alienated or even mocked and humiliated by children.

As a sign of respect, elders should be served first at all times during public and social gatherings. Their needs should be taken care of by younger ones with special care and respect. This is the way our human world should function with a sense of respect, ethics and compassionate responsibility in caring for each other.

Being Loyal and Consistent in Relationships with Relatives and Friends

The quality of relationships with your relatives and friends is more important than the number of relatives and friends you have. It is ethical to keep the old friends while making new friends. A new friendship should not change the attitude toward old friends. There is a moral obligation to maintain old friendships no matter how many new friends you make over time. This consistency of relationships with relatives and friends is not an attachment. It is a moral obligation to cherish the value of friendships for the mutual spiritual and social benefits of everyone involved.

Relatives and friends are not just a decorative factor of your life, with whom you share worldly pleasures and happiness. Friends and relatives share a mutual selfless interest and can be counted on to provide support and help when the need is there. A good friend, especially, is someone who helps the growth of positive qualities in you by facilitating necessary conditions. Someone who shows up only when you are happy and things are going well with you, and never shows up when you need them or when you have some problems and difficulties is surely not a friend. Finding good friends for yourself and being a good friend to them, and then cultivating a sense of loyalty and consistency is what is meant by "being loyal and consistent in relationships with one's relatives and friends."

Avoiding the Influence of Bad Friends and Being Confident in Your Own Moral Judgment

A bad friend is someone who influences you to develop negative and unethical behaviors. You must avoid the influences of such bad friends at all times. If someone starts drinking, smoking, stealing, lying, deceiving and cheating because of what a friend is doing, that person is under the influence of a bad friend. A real friend would not encourage anyone to behave in a way that is destructive or unethical.

It is extremely important to build strong self confidence and the ability to act according to your own moral judgments of what is wrong and what is right, what should be cultivated and what should be discarded, what should be accepted and what should be rejected.

Friendship does not mean doing any and every thing that your friend wishes. Saying or thinking that a friend must agree with your thoughts or actions is not an indication of true friendship.

A true friend is someone who helps you develop good qualities, helps you make a right decision, helps you to move in the right direction and helps you avoid anything that is negative and dangerous for you. Always strive to be confident in your moral judgment and ethical capabilities.

Being Benevolent and Helpful to Your Neighbors and Neighborhood

You must cultivate an effort to make positive contributions to your local community and neighbors by working to improve their living conditions, security, peace, prosperity and harmony. You must avoid being selfish and must not cause problems and suffering to your local community and neighbors because of pursuing your own self interest. Whenever the opportunity arises, work for positive changes in your community. Observing this moral obligation will make you a better person and will also earn the praise and respect of your neighbors. Being helpful to others can be the most satisfying part of your life.

Being Honest, Humble and Sensitive Towards Others' Wishes, Needs and Inclinations

Honesty, humility and sensitivity are the most important factors of a good and ethical person. Possessing material riches, factual knowledge, high intellect and attractive physical appearance will not make you a good and ethical person. Those who lack honesty, humility and sensitivity will be dangerous and harmful to others because of their dishonesty, arrogance, lack of consideration and negligence. Material richness and intelligence must be backed by a simple good heart and a sense of consideration for others' well-being and inclinations.

Following the Examples of Good and Decent People

You must make sure to observe, study and follow the conduct of the most morally advanced members of society. The way that they interact with other people and the way they dedicate themselves to selfless social service serve as examples to anyone who aspires to become a better person.

Living a Moderate Life, Free from Extreme Means of Livelihood

Living a moderate life with simplicity, free from extremes, is important and necessary. Of course, you must have reasonable material necessities, such as shelter, food, clothing, medicine, transportation and other basic needs to keep your life and fragile body in good health, protected from external elemental forces.

However, goods acquired just for their luxury or through greed are meaningless and a source of immorality. Indulging in overconsumption and excessive materialistic greed certainly will not make you happy and more ethical, but will instead bring you fear, destructive selfishness, worry and self imprisonment in a fearful material world.

Cultivation of moderation in all activities (what you eat, drink, wear, in sexual activity and in procuring material objects) is indeed very necessary for the moral well-being of you and others. Moderation is a virtuous means to a peaceful and happy life, free from the wrong means of a livelihood that is negative both for yourself and others.

Avoid Being Jealous and Competitive Due to the Prosperity and Success of Others

Feelings of jealousy and competitiveness because of the prosperity and success of others causes unhappiness and leads to many unethical behaviors. You will not be able to build good friendships with jealousy and competitiveness. Lack of good friendships is one of the causes of loneliness and depression. An attitude of joy towards the accomplishments and good fortune of others can be one of life's great pleasures.

Always Speak Sparingly, with Gentle Words that are Soothing to All Listeners

Speaking only sensible and gentle words that are soothing to all listeners is ethically important and necessary. Maintaining a mindful silence when talking is not necessary, or when talking is of no use, is a true noble act.

Talk that is not relevant, necessary or is of no help creates only empty noise that is unpleasant and disturbing to all listeners. You should be mindful not to engage in such talk at any time. A noble silence is precious. It is a sign of interior fullness. Noisy, senseless talk is a sign of interior emptiness.

Fulfilling the Needs and Wishes of Others

What turns others into aggressive, violent and hateful enemies is the neglect of their needs and wishes—by us individually or the world at large. Our present day terrorism problems are largely due to the negligence of others' needs, wishes and rights by our governmental bodies.

Fulfilling others' needs and wishes, and securing others' rights, from the individual to the international level, is the only way to stop terrorism and political violence. Killing one terrorist by a forceful act only breeds more violence and hatred in the minds of many who never even thought of carrying out a violent or terrorist act.

Always bear in mind that fulfilling the needs and wishes of others and securing their rights is ethical human behavior. It is something to be cultivated with great care and effort.

Disregarding the needs, wishes and rights of others is unethical and inhuman behavior. The fulfillment of the needs and security of others is absolutely essential for peace and harmony at all levels in the world.

Becoming Good Human Beings Through Training in Moral Conduct

MORAL CONDUCT IS THE most important part of a good human being. Without the practice of morality there is no foundation for becoming a good human being.

The Proper Place for Ethical Training

The practice of morality is not a religious concept at all. It is a discipline that naturally facilitates the growth of all that is good and wholesome. Of course, there are some ethical principles that are associated with particular religions, such as eating or not eating particular foods, and those types of ethics should not be taught in public schools. Ethics, in general, have nothing to do with religion.

Ethical training is the basis for a happy and constructive human life. It is integral to improving the quality of every person, so that his or her outlook, behavior and way of living become constructive and wholesome.

The conflict concerning teaching ethics in public school in the U.S., where there is separation between the church and the state, is due to mistaking morality with religion. It is a big mistake. As a result, teaching morality is ignored from the very beginning grades, in spite of the fact that it is the most important part of education.

Our schools should not merely teach facts and practical skills, but should also teach children how to be warmhearted and ethical people. This means schools should encourage the basic good human qualities of ethics, compassion and a sense of respect for all living creatures. Teachers, parents, local political leaders, lawmakers and other governmental bodies should come together to develop plans to teach ethics in the public schools and other educational institutions. The study of ethics should be part of social science and social studies courses.

Once again, we should not mistake ethics for religion. Many atheists are more ethical than religious believers.

No matter what cultural background we have, what social institutions we belong to, ethics is equally important and necessary for social peace, happiness and harmony. We must not lose sight of the importance of ethics in a society that overemphasizes developing the intellectual. The electronic world of the 21st century is facing an ethical crisis and this must be addressed with universal effort.

The practice of ethics is all about internalizing a sense of rightness, goodness, justness, wholesomeness, truthfulness and mindfulness of right and wrong.

Summary of Ethics for Children (and Adults) for Practice in Everyday Life

1. Be kind, gentle and polite to all others.
2. Be respectful to elders, parents, teachers and learned ones.
3. Be helpful to your neighbors and local community.
4. Be aware of others' needs and wishes, and make an effort to fulfill them.
5. Be obedient to your parents and teachers.

CHAPTER 8

Formal Ethics of Pratimoksha

FORMAL ETHICS ARE A set of moral vows (precepts) that a person commits to voluntarily by participating in a formal religious ceremony conducted by a lama or a spiritual teacher. Formal ethical vows are taken in order to cultivate higher spiritual awareness and more wholesome deeds, rather than merely abstaining from negative actions of body, speech and mind. Formal ethical precepts must be taken based on a foundation of the sound and stable spiritual motivations of renunciation and Bodhicitta.

Even if you are not a monk or nun, it is extremely useful to have a set of formal ethical precepts or vows to guide you in your daily life to help you build good habits. Ethical guidelines and discrimination allow a person to distinguish right from wrong, beneficial from harmful, virtuous from non-virtuous, etc. Human beings can be very destructive and create large scale disasters if we do not have moral guidelines and discrimination concerning what should be cultivated and what should be discarded. For the effective practice of morality you must know how to limit sensory activities for momentary pleasures and instant gratification. Discernment reveals the actual cost of sensory gratification to you and to others. The practice of morality always involves choosing the course of action that is least harmful and/or most helpful.

This discussion of formal ethics can help you formulate your own set of vows.

Formal ethical discipline entails more than just restraint. It also entails the deliberate cultivation of virtue and other essential good qualities, such as love and compassion, humility, forgiveness, tolerance, patience and a sense of responsibility, commitment and involvement. When these values are present in your life, everything you do becomes a tool to benefit other living beings and a source of the real happiness. Formal ethics encourage the very qualities that bring real meaning and spiritual value to life. It is clearly a rewarding enterprise to take a set of formal ethical precepts and then to keep them with mindfulness and deliberate conscious effort.

Many of the psychological and emotional illnesses suffered by people living in the materialistic Western world, such as depression, self hatred, anxiety and other psychological problems, are the products of excessive materialism. It is important to know that materialism is not the most important part of human life. The true purpose of life is to train in spiritual evolution by bringing together a good heart and a wise mind.

Renunciation and Bodhicitta: Their Importance in Formal Precepts

Two important motivations along the path are renunciation and Bodhicitta.

Renunciation (*nihsarana* in Sanskrit) is the desire for release from the cyclic existence of Samsara. Samsara is the never ending suffering caused by delusions and karma, whose seed is within ourselves, not in the material world. There can be no true happiness or peace as long as a person is blindly bound to delusions and karma. In samsaric existence, a person misidentifies temporary sensory pleasures as being the source of true happiness. Our pursuit of happiness actually leads to increased pain and suffering because of our misguided efforts to gain happiness from sources that cannot truly lead to happiness.

Renunciation as a motivation comes when the mind realizes that happiness cannot be found in external material objects and that sensory pleasures are just a temporary relief from our ongoing state of dissatisfaction. As a result of the realization of renunciation, the mind no longer feels any attraction or admiration towards the external sensory world and no longer sees that world as a source of happiness. True happiness can be found only within the individual. In brief, renunciation is a committed desire to be released from any sense of clinging to samsaric existence. Renouncing attachment to the material world does not involve a nihilistic denial of what is useful for our conventional needs. It is rather a fundamental shift away from materialism and towards seeking our ultimate happiness at its true source—inner spiritual development.

The Sanskrit word *Bodhicitta* means the mind of Enlightenment. It is the highest form of spiritual intention: striving for

Enlightenment for the sake of all sentient beings, without exception. Universal compassion is the root of Bodhicitta. A compassionate understanding of the unbearable sufferings of Samsara creates an urgent force to attain Enlightenment in order to be fully able to alleviate suffering.

Renunciation and Bodhicitta each has the lofty goal of reaching Nirvana and Enlightenment, and therefore these two motivations are very farsighted. The farsightedness involved in choosing the motivations of renunciation and Bodhicitta make the precept holder sound, strong, stable and fully determined to reach his or her ultimate goal. This stable and determined motivation makes spiritual practice very effective and consistent and makes progress significantly quicker.

A prospective monk or nun should carefully examine their motivations before taking formal ethical precepts. A person should not take formal ethical precepts and become a monk or nun to avoid having to work at a worldly job for a living. Also, it is wrong to take formal monks' and nuns' vows merely to avoid the difficult life of a householder with a heavy family responsibility. Anyone who takes formal ethical precepts simply to avoid having to work at a worldly job for a living, and does not make the commitment for any higher special purpose, only creates an extra burden for the community and the world at large.

Our historical Shakyamuni Buddha did not become a monk by taking formal ethical precepts just to avoid having to work at a worldly job for a living or to avoid the financial headaches involved in raising a family. He became a monk with the sincere motivation of renunciation and Bodhicitta and the sole goal of obtaining Enlightenment for the benefit of living beings who are confused, frustrated and painfully stuck in the samsaric mud without any rescuer.

An Ethic of Individual Liberation

Pratimoksha in Sanskrit (*so-sor tharpa* in Tibetan) means individual liberation. Individual liberation is a set of formal moral vows taught by the Buddha in his *Vinaya* teachings on morality and the monastic ethical code. Vinaya teachings and their associated practices are crucial for the teachings and practices of meditation and the understanding of interconnectedness of all things.

There are thirteen volumes of teachings on Vinaya that were directly taught by the Buddha. Later, the great Indian sage Acarya Gunaprabha wrote an extensive commentary on Vinaya Sutra called *The Roots of Vinaya Sutra*. This commentary became the primary study source of Vinaya among the Buddhist monastic institutions and Buddhist academic universities around the world.

In general, there are eight classes of formal ethical precepts of individual liberation, which are based on an individual's capability to keep certain sets of vows, given their lifestyle and external living conditions.

Within the formal ethical precepts of individual liberation, there are two basic divisions: those who live a householder's life, in a **lay community** rather than a **monastic sangha community**, those who have left a householder's life to become a monk or a nun.

If a person is capable of maintaining chastity for a lifetime, that person can leave the household and take monastic vows. If the person is not capable of maintaining chastity but can keep other vows, that person can take certain sets of lay person's vows that last an entire lifetime, or other sets that last for only twenty-four hours.

The eight classes of individual liberation precepts are:

1. Fully ordained monk precepts
2. Fully ordained nun precepts
3. Novice monk precepts
4. Novice nun precepts
5. Probationary nun precepts
6. Layman precepts
7. Laywoman precepts
8. One-day ordination precepts

All of the eight classes of individual liberation must be taken with renunciation as their prime motivating factor, or else committing to the ethical precepts of individual liberation is not an effective practice on the spiritual path.

All of the precepts of individual liberation lead to useful contentment and simplicity of life. The proper practice of formal ethical precepts of individual liberation requires training in mindfulness and maintaining a conscious effort to limit a person's needs and sensory activities for temporary pleasure and instant gratification. The mindful practice of limiting needs and distracting sensory indulgences naturally brings a sense of contentment. Mindful attention given to the cultivation of the inner causes for joy, happiness and satisfaction can help every individual to meet with the real purpose of life.

Monastic Precepts of Individual Liberation

The monastic precepts are extensive and may seem irrelevant to lay practitioners. This is not the case. The Buddha taught all of the precepts for moral and spiritual development; each contains important lessons for improving the condition of the world as well as gaining personal happiness. It is also the case that respecting the precepts that are faithfully kept by monastics enables us to learn from their good example of ethical conduct.

The first of the eight classes of individual liberation precepts is the fully ordained monk's precepts. Fully ordained monks take 253 precepts to be observed for his entire lifetime. The 253 precepts are categorized into two groups: the root precepts and the secondary or minor precepts.

The difference between the root and secondary precepts is that the transgression of root precepts cannot be purified, or corrected, without exception, in the presence of the sangha community,[1] whereas the transgression of secondary precepts can be purified in the presence of the sangha. This means that a monk or nun who commits a root transgression falls from monastic life and is not allowed to ordain again in this lifetime.

Generally speaking, killing includes even the smallest insect. However, the killing that breaks the root precept is the killing of a human being. All types of stealing constitute breaking the root precept of not stealing. Lying includes all types of consciously telling untruths, but the lying that breaks the root precept is lying about one's spiritual realizations and higher psychic powers.

Sexual activity that constitutes breaking the root precept is making direct contact between male and female genitals with the motivation of sexual desire and fantasy.

The other, secondary precepts include such things as not emitting sexual fluid while awake for sexual gratification, or not speaking sexually provoking words, not arranging the meeting

---

[1] A minimum of four fully ordained monks of the sangha community.

of men and women for sexual purposes, not sexually touching a female for tactile sensation, not causing division within the monastic sangha community, not causing a lay person to lose their devotion and faith in ordained monks and nuns, not engaging in too many worldly activities, not indulging in mundane householder's matters, not indulging in intoxicant substances, not keeping too many unnecessary and unused things in one's possession, and not eating in the afternoon, and so forth. All together there are 249 secondary formal ethical precepts of individual liberation. All of the formal precepts are proscribed precepts rather than prescribed precepts.

In general, many of the things proscribed by the secondary precepts, such as eating in the afternoon, are not negative by nature but become negative to an individual because they have been proscribed to that particular person for his or her spiritual benefit.

The precept of not eating in the afternoon can still be met by eating whatever is served and available without demanding, *I want this particular food and that*, and by being satisfied with the food that serves to sustain one's fragile body rather than desiring the deliciousness of certain kinds of food. This is the training that leads to contentment regarding food.

The precept of being limited to a few sets of robes is met by choosing robes that are only made from inexpensive fabrics, with very few choices of color, made of cloth that protects the body from external elemental threats and a design that represents one's culture. This limitation in dress is the practice that leads to contentment regarding clothes.

The precept about being satisfied with a small, simple and inexpensive shelter leads to contentment regarding shelter. An elaborate home with expensive furniture and other interior decorations is forbidden. Many of the formal ethical precepts of individual liberation are designed to lead to abandonment of unnecessary mundane quests for bigger, better, elaborate, decorative, expensive, and multiple houses, cars, boats, TVs, computers, clothing, and too many choices in food and other enjoyment. As a result of abandonment of the never ending quest for unnecessary worldly things, a person will naturally have extra time, energy and a calm state of mind with which to concentrate on spiritual practices of meditation and wisdom with stability and consistency. A sense of contentment in a person's life is extremely important for a successful spiritual quest. The sense of contentment comes from the practice of being happy with what is available to one's life instead of being constantly unhappy about what is not available in one's life.

The formal ethical precepts of individual liberation are all about reducing worldly activities and involvement in trying to meet never ending needs and depthless desires and greed.

Contentment is an inner source of joy and happiness. Lack of contentment—which really amounts to greed—sows the seed of envy and aggressive competitiveness, and leads to a culture of excessive materialism. In the culture of excessive materialism, one will see the success in obtaining material objects as the only true meaning and purpose of human life.

As a result, one will face a great deal of social and cultural pressure to be successful in gaining material wealth. External appearance and appropriate possessions and social status become everything in the eyes of the materialistic world.

Many of the psychological and emotional illnesses suffered by people living in the materialistic Western world, such as depression, self hatred and other psychological dysfunctions, are the side effects or symptoms of the culture of excessive materialism and capitalism. It is important to know that materialism or capitalism is not the meaning and purpose of human life. The true meaning and purpose of human life is to train in spiritual evolution by bringing together a good heart and a wise mind.

The second class of individual liberation precepts is fully ordained nun precepts. The fully ordained nun has eight root precepts and approximately 356 secondary precepts. Altogether there are approximately 364 precepts to be observed during her entire lifetime. One of the root precepts that is unique to a female monastic is not to sit or lie down in a manner that is sexually provocative either to herself or to an observer.

Some secondary precepts for the ordained nun include not engaging in obscene talk that leads to lust and depravity, not using cosmetic makeup and other forms of artificial beautification and not engaging in actions and behaviors that cause sexual temptation in others.

The third class of individual liberation precepts is for novice monks. The novice monk has four root precepts and thirty-two secondary precepts, for a total of thirty-six. One cannot be fully ordained as a monk until reaching at least the age of twenty. There are two reasons for this. First, a person below the age of twenty is not considered to be fully mature or capable of making responsible decisions. Second, from the Buddhist philosophical and metaphysical point of view, gender is not definitely established until the age of twenty.

The fourth class of individual liberation precepts is that of the novice nun. The novice nun has the same thirty-six as the novice monk.

The fifth class of individual liberation precepts is for the probationary nun. The probationary nun has forty-eight precepts. The probationary period lasts at least two years.

Lay Precepts of Individual Liberation

The sixth class of individual liberation precepts is layman precepts. *Upasaka* in Sanskrit means ordained layman. An ordained layman has only five precepts. All are considered to be root precepts. They are: not killing, not lying, not stealing, not indulging in sexual misconduct and not taking alcohol and other mind altering substances. However, a layman can take any one of the five precepts and be considered an *ekakarina Upasaka*, which means observing only one of the five vows. Taking all five vows is considered to be the highest and most complete expression of commitment to individual liberation by a layperson.

The seventh class of individual liberation precepts is laywoman precepts, *Upasika* in Sanskrit. An ordained laywoman also has the same five precepts as the above layman precepts. She can take one of the five vows and still be an ordained laywoman. Taking all five is again considered to be most beneficial.

The five layperson precepts taken for one's lifetime are:

1. Not killing
2. Not stealing
3. Not engaging in sexual misconduct
4. Not lying
5. Not using intoxicating substances

The last or eighth class of individual liberation precepts is one day ordained precepts. *Upavasa* in Sanskrit means a one day vow holder who is either a layman or a laywoman. An Upavasa vow holder has eight precepts, all considered root precepts. They are:

1. Not killing
2. Not stealing
3. No sex
4. Not lying
5. Not taking alcohol or other intoxicants
6. Not singing and dancing
7. Not eating after noon
8. Not using high and luxurious seating, beds and mattresses.

Not using perfume, jewelry and other cosmetic items and adornments are included in those eight precepts.

Purification Practice

Broken precepts can and should be confessed and purified. The purification process requires the aid of four powers. These are:

1. The power of **regret**
2. The power of **support**
3. The power of **resolution**
4. The power of the **remedy** or **antidote**

These are explained in the book, *Refuge* (see the subsection "Purification of Negative Deeds" in Chapter 10, "The Negative Actions to Be Avoided"). For further guidance, it is also wise to consult with a qualified spiritual teacher.

*Ethical conduct must begin
with the individual
and then extend outward
to influence the larger world.*

The Source of Immoral Conduct: Negative Thoughts and Emotions

FOR THE PERFECTION OF ethics, self control must be highly developed through mindful training in recognizing the delusional thoughts and emotions that motivate negative actions of body, speech and mind. If self control is not very highly developed, you will not notice the negative thoughts until you are at the point of killing, stealing and sexual misconduct, etc.

You may be sitting still, meditating, and suddenly a mosquito lands on your hand and starts to bite. You feel the pain, and your reaction is so quick, your level of awareness is so dull, you do not notice that you are about to do a wrong action till your hand is raised, ready to kill the mosquito. If you do become aware at that moment of what you are about to do, you can restrain yourself from killing. It is the same with stealing, sexual misconduct, lying, harsh speech, and so forth.

You must firmly resolve that you will not kill even the smallest insect under any circumstances. Killing should not be the first choice for resolving a situation. You can strengthen your resolve against killing if you reflect on the karmic effects of such an act. You have gone through lives beyond counting where you have killed and have suffered for killing. If you are to escape from this vicious cycle, you must put an end to killing from now on. No amount of physical pain and discomfort in this life can equal one moment of the suffering that will result in future lives if you do not stop killing right now.

The greatest aid in refraining from committing negative actions of body, speech and mind will be learning how to control the five senses. This means exercising as much control as possible over the things you pay attention to. The more control you have over what you see, hear, smell, taste, touch and think, the better will you be able to lead a moral life.

You can control your senses by reflecting on the fact that the second moment of a sensual pleasure is less satisfying than the first moment. This means that the subsequent moments of any sensual pleasure decrease automatically after the first moment. Therefore, the sensory pleasures cannot be increased by repeated indulgence.

The practice of ethics will not be effective if you do not learn how to control the senses in daily life.

Many of the emotional conflicts that are experienced by people all over the world can be resolved by establishing inner discipline through the cultivation of morality.

CHAPTER 10

Benefits of Individual Liberation Ethics

THE BENEFIT OF ETHICS is the ability to mindfully eliminate many harmful activities. Mindfulness directly helps to promote inner virtuous qualities of love, compassion, tolerance, respect, forgiveness and responsibility. It prevents you from being born into lower realms of miserable living conditions. It creates an inconceivable amount of merit and positive karma in the realm of worldly achievements, as well as beyond ordinary worldly achievements.

Ethics makes you beautiful, internally and externally. You will be well respected by others.

The mindful practice of ethics creates peace and harmony in and around you, and whoever is around you will gain profit from it. Others will naturally find peacefulness, safety, security and protection in your presence. Ethics brings the sense of simplicity, contentment, clarity of mind and a sense of deep concern for the well-being of others. It makes your prayers and service to others strong and effective.

Those who have taken formal ethical precepts, or vows, are more devoted to the service to others through prayers and active work in social institutions. There are common similarities among the ethical tenets of the major world religions. Christian monks and nuns are especially dedicated to social service in the fields of education, health and material prosperity. The evident ethical values shown by these monks and nuns in their charitable spiritual service to others is useful as an admirable role model for mankind. The goal, purpose and benefits of ethical precepts are more or less the same whether one takes formal religious precepts based on the concept of God or the concept of karma.

Forgiveness, patience and sincere observation of the law of karma are real values of morality. Buddha said that patience and inner refraining from negative action are the highest form of asceticism, and through them one can reach *moksha*, or liberation. Nagarjuna, an Indian philosopher who was the founder of the Middle Path school of Mahayana Buddhism, said *Physical asceticism is of no use, whereas mental asceticism is necessary.* So, constant effort should be undertaken to engage in the mental asceticism of refraining from the negative thoughts and emotions that drive harmful actions.

Formal religious precepts help to enhance your ability to help others and to end your tendency to harm others. Restraining from harming others is the essence of the initial stage of living the teachings of morality. An ethical life builds the foundation for the construction of all that is good, wholesome and beneficial.

Summary for Practice in Everyday Life

1. Be aware of your attachments to food, drinks, clothes, shelter and other enjoyment objects and adopt a conscious practice of contentment and moderation. Be satisfied with a moderate lifestyle which meets basic needs for food, clothing and shelter.

    Use your time, energy and effort for meditation so that you can enjoy inner peace. Practice purification so that you can enjoy the inner cleanliness that comes from acknowledging and purifying previous misdeeds. Practice accumulation of merit so that in the future you can enjoy living in an environment that is conducive to spiritual growth.

2. Do not cause harm and injury to others, including your enemies. Do not develop extreme attachment to your friends and loved ones.

3. Always bear in mind that your relationship with others is temporary and is based on temporary circumstances. Good friends can be bitter enemies by tomorrow, and a bitter enemy can become a helpful friend by tomorrow. So, the designation of friend or enemy is based on how others are affecting your life in the present moment. An extreme attachment to your friends and loved ones cannot make them permanent friends and loved ones. A hateful feeling and aggression towards your enemy cannot resolve the problem.

4. Be humble, honest, sincere and respectful at all times.

5. Avoid harmful activities of body, speech and mind in and under any conditions.

6. Cultivate wholesome deeds and actions with your best efforts and be friendly with everyone.

The Ethics of a Bodhisattva

A BODHISATTVA IS A person who truly cherishes others more than him or herself, and who is dedicated to being available for the needs of others at all times. The primary practice of a Bodhisattva is to restrain from selfishness or self-centeredness, always making sure to live with a deep concern for the well-being of others and a readiness to help them, even if there is great personal loss.

The effective practice of Bodhisattva ethics cannot happen without extensive training in the ethics of individual liberation. Therefore, there is no point in taking Bodhisattva vows without having a strong grounding in individual liberation vows, which mainly refrain from harming others. Merely not harming others requires no action, whereas the practice of Bodhisattva vows involves taking action to help others while also doing no harm. This cannot happen without overcoming the instinctive habit of cherishing yourself more than others and the instinctive tendencies to be harmful.

The painful process of overcoming a self centered mind and cultivating the practice of joyfully helping others with a consistent unbiased attitude at all times is the heart of Bodhisattva ethics. It is also the focus of this chapter.

How Can a Person Cultivate an Other-Centered and Other-Cherishing Attitude?

It is possible to cultivate an other-concerned and other-cherishing attitude by understanding that you are equal to and the same as all others. Every person wants to be happy and to overcome pain and suffering, just as you do. Every person has the right and freedom to be happy and to overcome pain and suffering, just as you yourself do. The right and freedom to be happy and to overcome suffering is a fundamental entitlement of life. Happiness is an inborn right of all living beings without distinction between the self and others, as stated in the Lama Chopa, in the Guru Devotion text:

> *Since no one wishes even the slightest suffering, or is ever content with the happiness they have, there is no difference between myself and others.*

> *May I be blessed to make others happy and to help them overcome their suffering and the causes of suffering.*

When you sincerely and honestly contemplate the meaning of this prayer, your whole perception and state of mind can be transformed into one of love, compassion and equanimity. Many practitioners find this prayer extremely powerful and useful for transforming in a short time any negative feelings and biased attitudes into positive feelings and unbiased attitudes.

True equanimity, love and compassion are mandatory for the cultivation of Bodhicitta. Bodhicitta is a pure state of mind in which others are held as more precious and cherished than oneself. The practitioner is decisively committed to becoming fully enlightened in order to be able to help all living beings at all times.

There are two practical methods for the development of Bodhicitta. There is the method of exchanging and equalizing self with others, and the method of sevenfold cause and effect.

Exchanging And Equalizing Self With Others

The method of exchanging and equalizing self with others is explained in *A Guide to the Bodhisattva's Way of Life,* written by the great Indian sage Shantideva. The method of sevenfold cause and effect is explained in the *Ornament of Clear Realization,* written by the Maitreya Buddha, who is believed to be the fifth or next historical Buddha. Shakyamuni Buddha was the historical Buddha of the present age and the fourth Buddha among the one thousand Buddhas of this golden era.

Buddhists believe the Maitreya Buddha will appear on our earth 2500 years from today. This has been foretold by many enlightened beings. A relevant prayer to make from your heart at the end of your daily practice is: *May this merit I have attained become a cause for all beings to be born before the feet of Maitreya*

Buddha. Also, because you may fail to become enlightened during the time of Shakyamuni's teachings (which still have 2500 years to go), you must do every possible preparation to be able to be present during the time of Maitreya Buddha.

The practice of the method of exchanging and equalizing self with others involves first understanding that we are the same as all other people, with an equal right to be happy and free from suffering. Then gradually we see that self-cherishing should be replaced with the cherishing of others.

You can change from self-cherishing to cherishing others by reflecting on the advantages of training the mind to cherish others and the disadvantages of the self-cherishing mind. Here are some useful quotations taught by the following enlightened beings:

Buddha Shakyamuni said, *All the sufferings and evils in the world arise from nowhere else but the evil thoughts of cherishing oneself.*

Shantideva said, *That which brings all evils and causes for unhappiness is the demon of the self-cherishing mind. How can we remain happy if we let this demon to dwell in our hearts?*

Lama Tsongkhapa said, *Cherishing oneself is the source of all loss. Cherishing others is the source of all gain.* And similarly, he said, *Since cherishing oneself is the doorway to all torment, while cherishing one's mothers (all other sentient beings) is the foundation of all that is good, I seek your (Guru Shakyamuni) blessings to make my core practice the yoga of the exchange of self with others.*

Sevenfold Cause And Effect

The second method for developing Bodhicitta is the sevenfold cause and effect. First, you focus on the facts supporting the beginninglessness of the cycle of rebirth time and again. Then, you realize that all living beings have been your kind mother at some time in the past. Finally, you recall their kindness, love, affection, caring, nurturing and protecting in all those limitless lifetimes.

You should contemplate the kindness of all living beings, and the fact that each one at some time has been your kind mother, until you develop true love, compassion and a special attitude of taking full responsibility to help them. With this loving feeling for all living beings and with great compassion for their limitless suffering, a Bodhisattva then makes a full commitment to become a Buddha for the ultimate service of others.

To summarize, the sevenfold causes and effects for the development of Bodhicitta are:

1. Recognizing all sentient beings as one's mother
2. Recalling their kindness
3. Realizing the need to repay their kindness
4. Feeling love for all beings
5. Feeling compassion for all beings
6. Developing the special attitude of taking full responsibility to help all beings
7. Developing the Bodhicitta intention of making the full commitment to become a Buddha in order to be of ultimate service to others

You must meditate on each of the first six factors in order to gain a strong and stable understanding that creates Bodhicitta.

Meditating on each factor requires thoughtful analysis, which will deepen your understanding and cultivate a feeling of closeness and intimacy towards all sentient beings, without exception.

Meditating on each of the sevenfold causes and effects is necessary because equanimity, love, compassion and Bodhicitta are based on valid reasons, and should not be based on emotion or personal judgments. Any feeling of closeness and intimacy towards others that is based on emotion and superficial reason will not be anything other than desire and attachment. Such feelings will be limited to certain people under certain circumstances.

For instance, you should not think the overwhelmingly strong feelings of romantic infatuation are an example of true love. The feeling of closeness and intimacy that is based on emotion cannot be the true love and compassion that are the mandatory tools for the development of Bodhicitta.

You can develop Bodhicitta in a very gradual way by slowly perfecting the meditation on each of the first six factors in their sequential order, Meditation is key. Without meditation there is not much opportunity in life to experience the profoundly calm and focused mental state which is needed to gain higher spiritual realizations and higher human positive qualities.

When you are meditating on love and compassion, you are not just using the love and compassion as a focal point. Rather you are transforming your entire mental state into one of love and compassion and holding that state for a longer and longer period of time.

Tong-len Taking and Giving Practice

There is a special practice to enhance the feeling of love and compassion towards others. It is called *tong-len* in Tibetan.

Tong-len means giving and taking practice. It is clearly described in Lama Chopa or the Guru Devotional Prayer:

> *In order to release all sentient beings from the vast ocean of samsaric existence,*
> *I seek your (Guru Shakyamuni) blessings to become adept in Bodhicitta.*
> *Through a pure unselfish wish, love, and compassion, conjoined with a meditative technique of mounting,[2]*
> *Lovingly giving and compassionately taking, upon the breath.*

The practice of giving involves the generous act of lovingly giving all your fortunes, merits, virtue and prosperity to others without the slightest concern for what will be left for you to use and enjoy. The practice of taking involves the compassionate act of taking others' misfortunes, karmic obstructions, pain, suffering and external and internal hindrances upon oneself without the slightest feeling of discomfort or uneasiness.

This practice, called tong-len, though difficult, is an extremely powerful and effective way to increase and deepen your love and compassion. There may not be a direct physical effect or impact on others, but certainly there will be a direct effect on your feeling of love, compassion and Bodhicitta, and that will greatly accelerate your spiritual practice toward Enlightenment.

---

[2] Mounting here refers to conjoining the breath in meditation with giving and taking.

Two Types of Bodhicitta

There are two types of Bodhicitta. One is called Wishing Bodhicitta and the other is called Engaged Bodhicitta. It is not necessary to take Bodhisattva vows in the case of Wishing Bodhicitta, but you must actually take Bodhisattva vows as a part of the Engaged Bodhicitta.

Acarya Shantideva said in his writing, *A Guide to the Bodhisattva's Way of Life:*

> *Bodhicitta, the awakening mind, in brief, is said to have two types: First, Wishing Bodhicitta in intention; then committed Bodhicitta, practical engagement. Wishing Bodhicitta is the pure cherishing of others and the wish that they be happy and free from suffering, while Engaged Bodhicitta takes the further step of being willing and committed to do whatever is necessary to help others, without regard for oneself.*

Eighteen Root Bodhisattva Precepts

The primary Bodhisattva precepts are twofold: the eighteen root precepts and the practice of the six perfections with the motivational factors of great compassion and Bodhicitta.

1. Not to praise oneself and belittle others
2. To give material aid or teachings of Dharma
3. To forgive when someone asks for forgiveness

4. Not to abandon the teachings of the Mahayana[3] vehicle
5. Not to misuse offerings made to the Three Jewels of Refuge
6. Not to abandon the Dharma
7. Not to cause the disrobing of monks and nuns
8. Not to commit any of the five acts of immediate retribution
9. Not to hold wrong views based on one's own false assumptions
10. Not to destroy places of worship or pilgrimage
11. Not to teach emptiness to immature recipients
12. Not to turn people away from working towards Enlightenment
13. Not to abandon the vows of individual liberation
14. Not to lie about attainment of higher spiritual realizations and psychic powers
15. Not to mistreat the teachings of the lower vehicle (Hinayana)
16. Not to misuse property that is dedicated for religious purposes
17. Not to engage in or support wrong ethical conduct
18. Not to give up the mind of Enlightenment

---

[3] One becomes a Hinayanist if his or her spiritual motivation is merely to attain Nirvana or individual liberation from delusion through the force of renunciation. However, even if such a practitioner reaches Nirvana, the subtle attachment to self remains intact.

One becomes a Mahayanist if his or her spiritual motivation is to attain Enlightenment for the sake of all living creatures. This desire to win Enlightenment not ultimately for oneself but for the benefit of all beings is called Bodhicitta. For more, see Appendix A, "The Two Fundamental Buddhist Schools."

The root precepts of Bodhicitta are broken if you indulge in the opposite of any of those eighteen root precepts. For example, praising yourself, belittling others, not giving material help or teachings of Dharma, not forgiving when someone asks for forgiveness, mistreating the teachings of lower vehicles, lying about the attainment of one's higher spiritual realization and misusing religious property, etc.

The Six Perfections

The six perfections are the actual practice of a Bodhisattva. They are as follows:

1. **Giving** – Giving material help such as food, clothing, medicine, shelter and other basic needs for survival. Giving Dharma teachings and other professional skills to make others' means of living easier. Giving love, affection, emotional comfort and protection from fear.

2. **Morality** – The mindful practice of putting others before yourself and protecting your mind from falling into self-cherishing attitude.

3. **Patience** – Voluntarily enduring the hardships and difficulties of spiritual practices and helping others over a long period.

4. **Effort** – Joyful or delighted interest in the cultivation of virtuous deeds and selfless actions, as well as happily and energetically engaging in spiritual practices.

5. **Concentration** – The practice of stabilization meditation with one pointed focus.

6. **Wisdom** – The mind realizing interconnectedness of all phenomena and the impermanence of phenomena that are all produced by other causes and conditions.

The practice of the six perfections is the actual path to the attainment of Enlightenment. Therefore, they must be cultivated by bringing *upaya* (skillful means) and *prajna* (wisdom) into union. The practice of skillful means leads to the attainment of *rupakaya* and practice of wisdom leads to the attainment of *dharmakaya*. These terms refer to the bodies attained by fully enlightened beings. They are discussed in the appendix.

Not making serious effort to practice the six perfections in everyday life is another way of breaking the vows of engaged Bodhicitta.

In brief, you are breaking Bodhisattva vows if you are: not willing to help others, mindlessly hurting others, holding on to negative thoughts and emotions, not increasing the merit that facilitates the growth of Bodhicitta and wisdom, not seeking the opportunity to help others, rejecting others' requests for help, not cherishing the benefits of Bodhicitta, doing good in exchange for a reward, not putting others before self, not dedicating your merit to the cause of others' happiness, hesitating to help others when it causes you a loss, and not helping others if doing so does not give you an advantage. It is much more difficult to keep the Bodhisattva vows than the individual liberation vows because Bodhisattva vows mean actively helping others even though you could suffer a great loss. Keeping the Bodhisattva vows as a way to help others is proactive. Helping others and doing something more than merely not harming is much more difficult in many ways. Therefore, in order to take the Bodhisattva vows you must have a genuine feeling of great compassion and Bodhicitta intention. You cannot consider yourself a Mahayana practitioner if you do not have Bodhicitta or at least great compassion. If you do not have Bodhicitta or at least great compassion, then you surely are not qualified to take Bodhisattva vows.

However, you can definitely make a wish to be able to take Bodhisattva precepts in the future. You can call this *wish* a wishing Bodhicitta if the wish is genuine and sincere.

To be a Mahayanist means to have the intention to be a Bodhisattva, or to already be a Bodhisattva, who cares for others more than yourself and to make yourself available to help others without being reserved or constrained by worldly matters. Unfortunately, in these days people often argue about the Mahayana and Hinayana paths, claiming to be one or the other. Such people cannot even be considered true Buddhists, let alone Mahayanists or Hinayanists. If you are a true Mahayanist, you should not mistreat the Hinayana doctrines. The Buddha taught his truths in many ways in order to reach all sorts of people. All of the teachings are valid and lead to the same ultimate goal.

*Ethics makes you beautiful,
internally and externally.*

The Four Ways of Magnetizing Living Beings Towards the Dharma

THE CORE OF THE Bodhisattva vows is to provide ultimate help to others by introducing them to the Buddhist principles, or Dharma, which can help liberate them from the vicious cycle of birth and death. There are four ways to do so, known as *the four ways of magnetizing living beings*.

The first is to give what is needed, at the proper time, without hope of reward. Such an action not only pleases the other person at that particular moment by giving them what they need, but also gradually helps the person in need turn towards the Dharma.

The second way is to speak pleasant and soothing words. Speaking in a heartfelt, simple way is useful as well as soothing It is most important not to be deceptive or too intellectual.

The third way is to act according to what is really going on. To help people, you must know how to provide help according to their real needs, not just assume you know what those real needs are. Similarly, you must take into account the other person's level of understanding. You must adjust the teachings to the other person's spiritual maturity, ability to comprehend and the actual conditions of their lives. This is called acting in accordance with the conventional world. For example, a mother does not give her infant solid food even though it is extremely nutritious, because the infant could not swallow or digest it. Instead she gives the infant milk or other digestible soft food. As the child grows, she gives it food that is more and more solid, and when the child is old enough, she gives it real solid food.

The fourth way to magnetize sentient beings is living in accordance with what you're teaching. What you teach must match the way you conduct your own life. Then you can inspire others through your own action, behavior and state of mind.

For example, saying that drinking alcohol is bad while you yourself indulge in alcohol weakens your moral authority. In the same way, teaching others that getting angry and dwelling on it is negative while succumbing to anger yourself could make others think that anger control is an impossible task. The way you think, speak and live must really match with what you're saying. This is known as *living in accordance with what one teaches*. In other words, match your words and your deeds.

These four ways of magnetizing living beings are the best and truest means for bringing them into the ultimate help of Dharma, which liberates them from illusion and is the essence of the Bodhisattva precepts.

*If an action would help you
but cause others to suffer,
you must not do it.*

The Commitments of Training in Bodhicitta

THIS CHAPTER PRESENTS GUIDELINES for developing loving kindness in your heart.

Behaviors to Be Avoided

Do Not Project Your Faults and Mistakes onto Others

Refrain from minimizing your own faults and mistakes, or projecting them onto others. You must honestly acknowledge your faults. Make a sincere apology to anyone you have harmed, and resolve to do better. It is very unethical to blame your faults and mistakes on others. This will never resolve a problem. Instead, it only creates more problems and creates confusion.

Do Not Misuse the Dharma for Power and Position

The Dharma, or Buddhist teachings, must not be misused to gain wealth, possessions, fame, power and control over others. Misuse of the Dharma or the prestige and moral authority it can give to a teacher is immoral and unethical. Such misuse will inevitably lead to disrespect for the teacher and the teachings. Using Dharma, power and social position to gain worldly pleasure, fame, wealth and control over others for one's own interest is surely immoral and unethical.

Religion, social position and power must be solely used for the benefit of peace, prosperity and harmony at all levels—from the local community to the universe.

Do Not Aim to Be the First to Get the Best

Do not try to get the best parts of what should be shared. For example, if a meal is going to be shared, you should not try to get the best and first parts of it for yourself. Avoid selfish behavior such as greedily cutting in front of a line, or expecting to get the biggest and best portion of the meal, or pushing into a crowded train or bus to get the best seat. Such behavior is morally wrong and inappropriate in the eyes of society.

Do Not Seek Happiness by Making Others Unhappy

There are ways of making others suffer for the sake of your own worldly gain and pleasure, such as killing, stealing, lying, engaging in sexual misconduct, slander and mistreating employees or deceiving employers. This includes hoping that one's parents will die soon so that one can inherit their property or wishing that someone would lose their job so that you can have it for

The Commitments of Training in Bodhicitta

yourself. There is a good chance you will be tempted to indulge in one of these unethical behaviors. As a moderate person, you must make full commitment to not seeking happiness by causing others unhappiness. It will be easier to make the commitment when you understand that personal happiness can never come from harming others.

The Lord Shakyamuni Buddha said:

He who seeks happiness
By hurting those who seek happiness
Will never find happiness.

Similarly, the great Indian yogi Shantideva said:

If I use others for my own purpose,
I will experience servitude.
But, if I use myself to make others happy,
I will experience happiness too.

There is a difference between the ways the wise and the ignorant seek happiness. The wise person seeks happiness by helping to make others happy, and naturally finds happiness, respect, praise and power. An ignorant person seeks happiness by making others unhappy, and therefore will never find true happiness.

People who seek happiness by causing unhappiness to others are foolish—not only because they cannot find true happiness that way, but also because they are the first victims of their own selfish actions by creating negative karma for the future. Through observation and contemplation you will see that seeking happiness at the expense of others is unethical and leads to the very opposite of what is desired.

Do Not Make a Promise You Cannot Keep

In general, people tend to make many empty promises, creating empty hopes, expectations and disappointment.

Making a promise is easy, but fulfilling the promise may be difficult. Before speaking, consider carefully the implications of your words and whether you can really make good on your promises. Disappointing others, especially in matters of Dharma knowledge and practice, is harmful because it will lead to people losing faith. It is very immoral to turn people away with empty hopes and expectations, and full of disappointment.

Do Not Wish for Gratitude

When you help others, do not expect anything in return. Helping others while expecting to be rewarded in some way turns kindness into a sham. This does not constitute helping others from the Bodhicitta perspective.

Do Not Think About Others' Faults

Do not dwell on the faults and imperfections of others. Instead, pay close attention to your own shortcomings. Most people pay close attention to others' faults and imperfections, and then fail to treat others with respect. People tend to pay close attention to their own good qualities, which can lead to an inflated ego and arrogance.

Thinking about your own knowledge and good qualities leads to conceit, but thinking about the good qualities and knowledge of others leads to wholesome minds filled with respect and affection.

Lord Shakyamuni Buddha said, *A person who is aware of his own faults and imperfections is indeed wise.*

Similarly, Atisha said, *Do not think of the faults of others; think rather of one's own faults and imperfections and make an effort to remove them.*

Do not think about your own knowledge and good qualities. Think rather of the knowledge and good qualities of others. In this way you should pay respect to others.

Do Not Offend Others

Do not disagree with someone with a hateful attitude. Likewise, you should not point out their mistakes or refuse to comply with their reasonable wishes. It is important to make an effort to cooperate with others' wishes and views, unless doing so would do some harm. To protect others' feelings and to comply with their wishes is extremely important. Make a commitment not to offend others at all times.

Do Not Retaliate for Verbal Abuse

Do not respond to anger with anger, harm with harm, and insult with insult. Not responding to anger with anger, etc. is one of the best ways to help others, because you are helping them to subdue their anger, helping them find calmness and peace of mind. If you respond with anger to those who speak spitefully, the anger of the other person will increase and this will cause them more emotional pain.

Do not retaliate unless there is good reason, such as the protection of a third party.

Essential Ethics

~~~

These are the behaviors you should avoid. Now we will turn to behaviors that should be cultivated and developed.

Behaviors You Should Encourage

Cultivate Equality Between Self and Others

One may do so by reflecting on this prayer:

> *Since no one wishes even the slightest pain or is ever content*
> *   with the happiness they have,*
> *There is no difference between myself and others.*
> *May I be blessed to strive towards making others happy.*

Cultivate a Genuine Feeling of Compassion

Heartfelt compassion desires to protect and secure everyone's natural right to be happy and overcome suffering. Make a conscious effort to provide help and protection for those in need without expecting personal reward.

Make a compassionate, conscious decision to become enlightened in order to provide ultimate help and protection to all sentient beings.

Renew your decision to become enlightened upon waking up in the morning and then resume your daily activities under the force of that renewed decision.

Practice for other's welfare by giving, patience, forgiveness, meditation, wisdom and compassionate concern for others.

Dedicate your merit and good deeds for the cause of attainment of Enlightenment without delay. Here is an example of a dedicational prayer:

> *By the merit I have accumulated through meritorious deeds,*
> *May all sentient beings attain full Enlightenment without delay.*
> *May I find each day as many opportunities to create merit*
> *As there are grains of sand in the ocean.*
> *May all who are sick and ill quickly be freed from their ailments.*
> *Whatever diseases there are in the world*
> *May they never occur again at any existing level.*

The Ethics of Tantra

THE PURPOSE OF THIS chapter is simply to briefly introduce the reader to this advanced stage of ethical conduct. Tantric, or esoteric, teachings are for a select few whose minds are karmically pure and who have highly developed spiritual maturity. A practitioner engages in tantra only when highly spiritually developed. Until then, one must concentrate on the practice of individual liberation and the Bodhisattva ethical conduct.

The core of tantric morality is transcending your ordinary perceptions of your body and mind into seeing yourself as embodying the highest qualities of wisdom and compassion. Not seeing anything as disgusting or unclean is a unique feature of tantric ethics.

There are fourteen root vows for the tantric practitioner. They must not be broken even if you break the two lower sets of vows, the individual liberation and Bodhisattva vows. In other words, you must do everything to protect the tantric vows even if that action causes you to break the individual liberation and Bodhisattva precepts.

The fourteen root precepts are:

1. Not to belittle one's tantric master or guru
2. Not to disregard the vows instructed by the Buddha
3. Not to speak badly of or criticize your relatives, tantra brothers and sisters
4. Not to give up love for sentient beings
5. Not to give up Bodhicitta motivation
6. Not to despise the Sutra (Buddha's discourses) and tantra teachings
7. Not to expose the secret of tantra to those who are not initiated
8. Not to mistreat your body
9. Not to be skeptical concerning emptiness (the interrelatedness of all things)
10. Not to associate with bad friends
11. Not to fail to reflect on emptiness
12. Not to undermine others' faith in Dharma
13. Not to fail to observe the pledges and commitments

The Ethics of Tantra

14. Not to despise (belittle or disrespect) women. That is because in tantra, the feminine energy is a critical element for speeding up spiritual realization.

In tantra, criticizing your guru and despising women are considered to be very serious negative acts. Criticizing your guru and despising women disqualify you as a tantric practitioner, and they cause you to go to vajra hell, the deepest realm of hell. You will be reborn there by the karmic force of breaking the tantric vows.

In tantra, the guru is considered to be the only source of blessing and women are considered to be the source of non-dual bliss and energy. Without female energy as the factor that activates the latent states of blissful awareness, thereby increasing the intensity of the experience of emptiness, a person cannot attain Enlightenment within a single lifetime.

The tantric precepts are primarily meant to keep your perceptions clean and pure in your own mind and in interactions with the world.

A person studies tantra only when spiritually qualified. Until then, you should emphasize the practice of individual liberation and the Bodhisattva moral conduct.

*The only way
to make Planet Earth
the peaceful and beautiful place
we all wish for is to
let all of our actions be guided
by ethics and compassion.*

Conclusion

WE'VE LOOKED AT HOW ethics is the universal basis for the generation of good qualities of body, speech and mind, without need of any particular religious affiliation or belief. Ethics and compassion are the fundamental excellent qualities of human beings.

Due to lack of ethics and compassion at all levels of human society, the global community is facing tremendous suffering from fear, distrust, conflict, war, crime, violence and a huge economic gap between the rich and poor that breeds anger and hatred. Ethics and compassion are more important than any belief held by any world religion. They have the greatest potential to solve the problems within our human family.

It is extremely important for all of us to put the highest value and emphasis on ethics and compassion, which are intimately related and mutually supportive. The way that modern culture stresses money and material possessions should be examined and challenged. We must recognize the importance of instilling truly beneficial values in our children, rather that empty materialistic values. Opening the hearts and minds of children to ethics and compassion is the highest priority of parenthood. The future well-being and happiness of children and their ability to make a positive contribution to the world will be based on the degree to which they have learned these values.

The only way to make Planet Earth the peaceful and beautiful place we all wish for is to let all of our actions be guided by ethics and compassion. Humans, other living beings, and the environment would then exist in peace, harmony and security from the individual to the global level.

Lord Buddha has said,

> *Ethics is the most precious inner wealth. It has the nature of cooling and soothing our burning desire, greed, attachment, lust, aversion and hatred. It is the most beautifying ornament, emanating all good qualities of mankind. It is the ultimate source of peace, happiness and spiritual development.*

Before passing into parinirvana, Buddha stressed the crucial importance of ethics by leaving these final words to his followers:

When I am gone, no one should be appointed in my place. Treat my teachings on ethics as your living teacher.

I hope that this book on ethics will help all types of interested readers to come to realize the importance of developing ethics and compassion as their fundamental inner qualities.

The Life of Buddha and His Fundamental Teachings

Buddhism

BUDDHISM CAME FROM AN enlightened human being. It did not come from a perfect, omnipresent, omnipotent and omniscient supernatural being or what is called *God*. The concept of God does not exist in Buddhism. However, there is the concept of a fully enlightened human being who has infinite compassion, wisdom and an omniscient mind.

Every such enlightened being is called a Buddha, or fully awakened one. Buddhahood is the highest spiritual realization that can be attained by human beings. All human beings have the potential to attain Buddhahood, with no exceptions regarding race, gender, culture, tradition, family or geographical location.

Buddha was an ordinary person like us before he became a Buddha. This shows us that every ordinary person can reach Buddhahood. Buddhahood requires both the elimination of all negative qualities (such as imperfections, delusions, obstructions and psychic limitations) and the development of positive qualities (such as perfect wisdom, compassion and the all-knowing psychic capabilities).

The path to Buddhahood is very slow; it might take eons, with progress over many lifetimes. Instant Enlightenment is impossible. Anyone who teaches the possibility of instant Enlightenment is delusional and deceptive.

Buddha's Birth and Early Life

The Buddhist teachings of our present era began with the historical Shakyamuni Buddha who is considered to be the fourth Buddha of this golden age or *kalpa*. The historical Shakyamuni Buddha was born about 600 years before Christ into a respected royal Hindu family in Lumbini, in the northern region of what was at the time India but is now Nepal. His name was Prince Siddhartha.

Soon after his birth, Siddhartha stood up, took seven steps and said, *I am the supreme being in this realm of existence*. His mother died seven days after giving birth. His mother's younger sister, Prajapati, took over as foster mother. Later, she became his father's second wife.

A holy *Brahmin* priest saw the baby and predicted that the baby would have a choice in later life of becoming either a powerful monarch or a great spiritual teacher. The priest said that the young prince would most likely renounce worldly concerns in order to search for a spiritual cure for the pain and misery that afflict all living creatures.

Growing up as a young prince, Siddhartha led a very sheltered life, enjoying every possible pleasure a royal life had to offer. Yet from early childhood he was very curious to know about the facts of real life and he had very strong latent psychic powers and high intelligence.

When he reached young adulthood, Siddhartha was able to escape the palace and his sheltered life and discovered the four facts of life that his family had tried to shield him from: old age, sickness, death and poverty. Seeing this suffering made him very sad, depressed and horrified. However, he also reacted with deep compassion and was determined to do what he could to end human suffering.

Buddha's Renunciation

Deeply moved by great compassion, Siddhartha vowed to seek Enlightenment—a state which would eliminate all suffering and the potential seeds of suffering. As an enlightened being he could then lead others to freedom. Siddhartha renounced the pleasures of the palace and became a monk at the age of twenty-nine.

At the time, he was married to Yushodhara and they had one son. Yet he left his home and family to search for a cure for the human suffering and pain that had deeply touched his compassionate heart. And so one night, giving his wife and son a last kiss as they slept, he left his home and family.

Siddhartha first went to live in a lovely forest with five other ascetics. He renounced sensual pleasures, and practiced extreme asceticism, with the goal of weakening the body in order to free the mind. After reaching the brink of starvation, however, he found that total denial of the body and its needs was not a solution. Although ordinary pleasures of the body and mind cannot bring lasting happiness, still the human body and mind must be healthy vehicles for the search for Enlightenment. The answer was a middle way—neither blindly indulging in the world of the senses nor denying its validity.

Buddha's Search for Enlightenment

After regaining his strength, Siddhartha sat in deep meditation under the bodhi tree at the town of Bodh Gaya. He made a promise not to rise from meditation until he had reached his ultimate spiritual goal of Enlightenment. Conventionally speaking, in his spiritual quest—from age twenty-nine when he left the palace until he sat down under the bodhi tree at age thirty-five—Siddhartha had intensively practiced meditation for six years, exploring the ultimate nature of reality.

He reached his ultimate aim when on the fifteenth day of the fourth lunar month, a day that fell on a full moon, he moved through three stages of spiritual realizations.

During the first watch of the night he acquired the power to look back through his previous existences, recalling them in full detail. In the second watch of the night he attained the clairvoyant power which allowed him to see the death and rebirth of all beings in the universe according to the karmic effects of their good and bad deeds. During the third watch of the night he attained the most profound meditative experience of what is usually translated as *emptiness*.

Emptiness can also be called *connectedness*. Buddhism teaches that every person and every object are connected and part of the same whole. There is nothing that can exist totally by itself without depending on something else other than itself.

Take, for example, a wooden table. It seems to exist all by itself. But there would be no table without the wood, and no wood without trees, and no trees without sun and water and earth, and so on down to atomic particles and energy. So even a simple table is connected to and made up of all these elements, and could not possibly exist without these complex physical constituents. This does not mean the table itself does not exist, and in fact we are encouraged to feel heartfelt appreciation for all those things in life we find useful and necessary.

However, when we cling to an identity of ourself as something individual and apart, we are mistaken and deluded. This mistaken sense of separateness can lead to envy, greed, insecurity, loneliness and a whole range of painful emotions.

Buddha's realization of emptiness destroyed the root of craving, clinging, grasping and ignorance at once and forever.

The fourth lunar month, *Saka Dawa* in Tibetan, is considered a very holy, spiritually sacred month for Buddhists because this is the month in which Buddha was born, reached Enlightenment, and passed away.

Enlightenment

Siddhartha sat in meditation for six years and gained the most profound, translucent and inexpressible spiritual experience. Later he called his spiritual realizations Enlightenment, or Buddhahood. Since then he has been called *Buddha*, because he reached the state of Buddhahood.

Enlightenment is a state of highest spiritual realization in which the perfection of abandonment—of every flaw, negative emotion, mental obstruction, psychic limitation—and the perfection of attainment—of infinite wisdom, compassion, and psychic capabilities—are fully achieved. There is nothing left that needs to be corrected and nothing left that needs to be realized.

Enlightenment is a state completely without imperfections, karma and the distorted thoughts and emotions that come from the failure to see true reality. Enlightenment permanently erases the sense of separation that creates psychological and emotional conflict between us and the world. Enlightenment is unconditionally blissful and free of all contaminations.

In short, Enlightenment is the ability to see things as they really are.

Buddha's Teachings

At first, Buddha was reluctant to teach about his realizations, because he thought others might not understand what he had to share from his experience of Enlightenment. His realization was beyond conception, beyond expression. How could such a profound view be confined within the bounds of mere words? Mystics from all traditions have struggled with this same dilemma. How to express the inexpressible?

Finally, after forty-five days spent pondering ways to teach all kinds of human beings, Buddha came out of seclusion. He devoted the next forty-six years of his life to teaching, and then passed away at the age of eighty-one.

He left brief instructions about what his followers should do with his body and also instructed that no one should be appointed as his successor since he never claimed to be anything but a compassionate teacher. He wanted his followers to study his teachings and put them into practice for themselves.

Buddha's teachings can be divided into three groups known as the *Tri-Dharmachakra*, or three rounds of teachings.

Buddha's first round of teachings was given at Sarnath, Varanasi, to the five ascetics who were his former companions in the search for true understanding. There he taught what are known as the Four Noble Truths. They are:

1. Life is suffering.
2. Suffering is caused by karma and delusion.
3. It is possible to end suffering.
4. There is a path to end suffering.

Thus, the first two truths describe our ordinary condition, while the third and fourth point to the enlightened state.

It is significant that Buddha did not immediately teach the ultimate reality that he had realized. Instead, he began with a description of ordinary life which we could validate or refute for ourselves through our own experience.

Throughout his teaching, Buddha emphasized that we should not blindly accept what he said without thorough examination. Blind faith is powerless and even useless to remove the delusions and obstructions that prevent us from experiencing reality.

Instead, relying on his guidance, we must come to realize each and every step on the path through our own personal experience.

The second round of teachings was given at Vulture Peak to an audience of Bodhisattvas, those who are driven to reach full Enlightenment in order to be of ultimate help to all other living creatures. Bodhisattvas realize that personal freedom from Samsara is not enough to lead others to freedom because personal freedom from Samsara still contains a subtle attachment to self and, thus, cannot be pure. At Vulture's Peak, Buddha taught about emptiness, the true but difficult concept that all phenomena are connected.

The third and final round of teachings was given at Yangpa Chen to an audience of *Cittamatra* philosophers, also known as the Mind Only school. This school sees reality as a mere reflection of the perceiver's mind, like the reflection of an object in a mirror. Since the reflection of an object cannot be found outside the mirror, this school says external phenomena cannot be found outside the perceiver's mind. Seeing the subjective mind and its object as having separate entities is a false duality. Here Buddha was discussing emptiness (or connectedness) in terms this group would understand, but these teachings are not the ultimate intended description of emptiness.

The Two Fundamental Buddhist Schools

Two fundamental Buddhist schools developed during Buddha's lifetime, the Hinayana and Mahayana schools. These two schools reflect different spiritual motivations of their practitioners and have nothing to do with geographical location, culture, tradition or racial or tribal group.

One becomes a Hinayanist if his or her spiritual motivation is merely to attain Nirvana or individual liberation from Samsara through the force of renunciation. However, even if Nirvana is reached by such a practitioner, the subtle attachment to self remains intact.

One becomes a Mahayanist if his or her spiritual motivation is solely to attain Enlightenment for the sake of all living creatures. This desire to win Enlightenment, not ultimately for oneself but for the benefit of all beings, is called Bodhicitta.

The difference between Nirvana and Enlightenment is that Nirvana is a state beyond ordinary existence, in which one merely overcomes the forces of karma and delusional obstructions. Enlightenment, however, is not only a state beyond ordinary existence, but it is completely free from subtle attachment to self, making possible the full Enlightenment of a Buddha.

Hinayana and Mahayana are not mutually exclusive teachings. The Hinayana teachings must be learned and practiced prior to training in Mahayana. The Mahayana goal of gaining Enlightenment with the motivation of Bodhicitta is impossible without being firmly grounded in the Hinayana practices. On the other hand, the Hinayana path alone cannot give birth to full Enlightenment without entering into the Mahayana path, motivated by Bodhicitta.

The Three Baskets of Teachings

The subjects of Buddha's teachings are grouped into three baskets or three higher trainings: first, **ethics**; second, **concentration**; and third, **wisdom** or penetrative insight.

The teachings are interrelated because in order to develop the wisdom to penetrate and understand the ultimate nature of reality, it is necessary to have a mind which is exceptionally well trained and supple.

Trying to analyze a subtle concept like emptiness with a disturbed mind is like trying to read by the light of a flickering candle. Therefore, developing wisdom requires deep meditative concentration which strengthens the mind and allows it to maintain a powerful single pointed focus. Likewise, trying to develop meditative concentration in a mind which is undisciplined, dissipating its energy in desires or aversions, would also be impossible.

Therefore, ethical discipline is the foundation for all higher realizations and perfections. Discipline is the seed of all that is good, constructive and beneficial in both the spiritual and the worldly fields.

The first basket of teachings concerns ethics, or the inner voluntary self-discipline of living in a wholesome way, without harming others.

Practicing ethics means consciously refraining from negative and destructive behavior. When we sincerely try to refrain from negative actions, our minds become calm and clear so that we feel happy and content. The practice of ethics also includes cultivating positive qualities. In addition to refraining from harm, we should make an active effort to help whenever possible.

In this way our behavioral patterns become supple, appealing, beneficial and non threatening to those around us. As a result, we contribute to a harmonious environment that creates greater happiness and peace.

The Sanskrit term for ethics is *shila*, and it literally means cooling and peaceful. When our minds are free from negative emotions, we become tranquil, relaxed, peaceful, which allows positive states of mind such as love, kindness, compassion and contentment to arise naturally. A sense of inner contentment brought by the mindful cultivation of positive actions is essential for inner spiritual development as well as for simply being happy with what is available to our life.

The second basket is the training in meditation. Meditation (or concentration) is a calm, peaceful state of mind which is free of the mind's usual busy activities of chasing after fantasies, thoughts and sensory experiences of pleasure and pain. The practice of meditation is an internal process of discovering and becoming familiar with our own mind and its creations. By practicing meditation we can develop insight into ourselves—into our emotions and thoughts and into their sources. This exploration of the mind is the practical aspect of Buddhism. It is the method by which we come to realize true reality, a realization which has the power to free us from the painful cycle of birth and death. A detailed explanation of meditation can be found in the book *Diamond Key for Opening the Wisdom Eye*.

The third basket of teachings is about wisdom, a well trained state of mind capable of fully realizing the ultimate truth of reality, which is emptiness (or connectedness). The realization of emptiness (*shunyata* in Sanskrit) is the ultimate antidote to our mental delusions and ignorance, which are the prime causes of our pain and suffering. A detailed explanation of the deep wisdom that sees the truth of reality can be found in the book *Two Subtle Realities: Impermanence and Emptin*ess.

Wisdom requires a crystal clear state of mind. A crystal clear state of mind requires training in meditation. Training in meditation requires developing ethics and morality by mindfully watching our actions with a commitment to refrain from negative or harmful actions.

Therefore, the practice of ethics is a crucial and essential practice for all further spiritual development, as well as for all that is conducive to happiness, peace and harmony in the world.

These three rounds of formal teachings are called Sutrayana, or exoteric teachings. Buddha gave these teachings publicly and every member of the audience, regardless of spiritual maturity, could understand them on some level. Buddha also gave the more complex and subtle teachings known as Tantrayana. Tantric or esoteric teachings were restricted to a select few whose minds were karmically purer and who had highly developed spiritual maturity.

Buddhism Respects Other Spiritual Paths

Buddhism does not criticize other religions and instead recognizes that people need to explore and practice according to the beliefs that suit their culture, disposition and other needs. Although the philosophy of another faith may not agree with the Buddhist viewpoint, if it benefits others it is worthy of respect. The following principles support this perspective:

1. Buddhism teaches love and respect towards others.
2. Buddhism teaches tolerance towards other religions and towards differing beliefs.
3. Buddhism does not proselytize but keeps an open door for anyone with an interest in Buddhism.

4. Buddhism does not include the concept of missionary work, but rather teaches giving compassionate care to anyone you encounter.

5. Buddhism stresses the development of discriminating wisdom and a good heart.

6. Buddhism emphasizes the right of choice and freedom in your beliefs.

7. Buddhism does not block or suppress the human intellect from searching for reality, but teaches various means and ways to use the intellect to search for reality without resorting to blind faith.

8. Buddhism teaches various logical avenues and meditative analyses to gain a lucid faith.

9. Buddhism does not teach that intellectual inquiry about God's message is disloyal or sinful, but rather teaches that intellectual inquiry is necessary to find the truth and to find the religious teachings that are in accordance with the results of your inquiries.

10. Buddhism does not encourage anyone to abandon their own religious tradition, but rather encourages them to learn from other religious traditions in order to deepen their own religious beliefs and understandings.

11. Buddhism does not incorporate a concept of heaven and hell based on whether or not you believe in Buddha. It does teach that you can end up in hell if you perform negative and immoral deeds and that you can go to heaven if you perform positive and moral deeds, both regardless of any belief in any being.

12. Buddhism teaches how to be respectful of religions and beliefs of other people.

13. Buddhism teaches various ways and means for the cultivation of inner salvation.

14. Buddhism teaches that every human being has enough spiritual resources within to make it possible to gain Enlightenment.

15. Buddhism does not teach how to be a believer but rather teaches how to be a goodhearted person.

16. Buddhism teaches that you should not consider killing, even though there may be great loss to your personal interest.

17. Buddhism teaches that it is wrong to sow seeds for religious disharmony by maintaining that what you believe in is correct and that others are wrong. Rather, it teaches how to be sincere and happy in your own religious belief without being unhappy and annoyed by the beliefs of others.

*Lord Shakyamuni Buddha said:
A person who is aware of
his own faults and imperfections
is indeed wise.*

Kayas

BUDDHA WAS ABLE TO teach ethical guidelines flawlessly because he himself had gone through the path of ethical attainment. In the process he developed the four *kayas*, which in Sanskrit means body or form. These are not physical bodies but more like holders or containers of spiritual achievements.

The four kayas are called *Sambhogakaya*, *Nirmanakaya*, *Svabhavakaya*, and *Jnanadharmakaya*. The first two kayas are created through the practice of benefiting others while not causing harm, either intentionally or unintentionally—not only during moments of meditation but when actively involved in the world. The second two kayas are created through the perfection of inner spiritual realization. Svabhavakaya holds the perfection of abandonment of all obstructions. Jnanadharmakaya holds the perfection of inner wisdom.

The second two kayas are inner tools used to help others find the correct path. They are expressed through the first two kayas. An explanation of the four kayas and the physical characteristics of a Buddha can be found below.

Each of those kayas has a different potential for benefiting other living creatures, who have different karmic predispositions and different needs, interests, inclinations and aspirations.

It is important for a student to know what a Buddha is, who the historical Buddha was, and how to achieve Buddhahood. It is also important to know the enlightened qualities of a Buddha, including the various types of kayas, which are a medium through which compassionate activities can reach living creatures. Unless we understand that a Buddha does not have the potential to lie or deceive through desire for personal gain, then it is impossible for us to joyfully accept Buddha as a teacher capable of taking us on the path of Enlightenment.

Here are the different bodies of a Buddha and how they are achieved through the merit of wholesome and ethical behavior.

What Is Sambhogakaya?

Sambhogakaya is a Sanskrit word that means complete enjoyment body or utility body. It is a most subtle Buddha body which cannot be perceived by an ordinary being but can be perceived by an Arya Bodhisattva, a superior Bodhisattva. An Arya Bodhisattva is one who has reached the third of the five paths, the path of seeing. This type of Buddha body is subtle, like a dream body, except it can create a shadow.

Sambhogakaya has five definite qualities:

1. Definite place of residence in the *blissful realm-below-none*. This realm is a richly adorned physical place that comes from the completion of the accumulation of merit. Merit is a positive spiritual energy that affects the external physical realm and environment.
2. Definite characteristics of the body. The Sambhogakaya body is always adorned with thirty-two major and eighty minor auspicious marks.
3. Definite length of time of existence. Living for as long as living creatures live in delusion.
4. Definite teachings. Always teaching Mahayana or Bodhisattvayana principles.
5. Definite disciples. Always teaching to a circle of Arya Bodhisattva disciples.

The Buddha body that possesses those five definite qualities is called Sambhogakaya, or complete enjoyment body. It is a source of a second type of enlightened body called Nirmanakaya.

What Is Nirmanakaya?

Nirmanakaya is also a form body. Nirmanakaya means emanation body. It emanates from the Sambhogakaya in a grosser physical form that is accessible to all ordinary sentient beings, enabling them to receive direct teachings of Hinayana, Mahayana and Vajrayana principles from an enlightened being.

The historical Shakyamuni Buddha is considered to be the Nirmanakaya of this *pradipa kalpa*. Pradipa kalpa in Sanskrit means the golden era or era of light. The golden era is a time in which the teachings are available as sunlight is available during the daytime.

Both the Sambhogakaya and Nirmanakaya (together called the Rupakaya or Buddha's physical body) have thirty-two major marks and eighty minor marks of a fully enlightened being. The purpose of the Nirmanakaya's thirty-two and eighty auspicious marks is to convince the conventional world that he or she is the historical Buddha of a particular golden era, and that there will be no other second Buddha who will appear as a historical Buddha to teach in that golden era.

Each one of the thirty-two and eighty marks comes from its own distinct spiritual causes of merit accumulated from the method aspect of the paths.

The method aspect of the path includes the following practices: deep appreciation and commitment in taking refuge, devotional faith/trust in the guru, generation of compassion and Bodhicitta, unselfish giving of material help and professional work skill, inner self-discipline of ethics with appreciation of karmic law, patience and forgiveness, joyous effort in consistently cultivating the path to Enlightenment, stabilizing meditation on the image of enlightened beings and their spiritual qualities, as well as many other meritorious actions.

What Are the Thirty-two Major Marks of the Buddha?

For each of the thirty-two marks there is a distinct cause derived from merit created during training in the causal path leading to Buddhahood:

1. The palms of the hands and feet bear the image of a wheel.

The cause for the wheel on his palms and under his feet is the merit caused from providing spiritual service to one's guru, such as doing his or her errands, providing transportation, making welcome and farewell events with a spiritual attitude and respect.

2. The feet are well set upon the ground like a tortoise.

The cause for his feet being well set upon the ground like a tortoise is merit created from keeping the three types of precepts unbrokenly until one reaches Buddhahood.

3. The fingers and toes are webbed.

The cause for his fingers and toes being webbed is the merit created from the practice of giving and the practice of the four skillful means of bringing others to Dharma.

4. The palms of the hands and feet are smooth and tender.

The cause for his palms and feet being smooth and tender is merit created from the practice of giving food, drinks and other basic needs with a respectful and humble manner.

Essential Ethics

5. The body has seven prominent features: broad heels, broad hands, broad shoulder blades and broad neck.

The cause of the body having broad heels, broad hands, broad shoulder blades and broad neck is merit created through the practice of providing excellent food and drink that soothe and completely satisfy others' desires and wishes.

6. The fingers are long.

The cause for his fingers being long is merit created from the practice of saving the lives of those in line to be killed or tortured.

7. The feet are soft.

The cause for his feet being soft is merit created from the practice of giving protection to others and supporting their wholesome means of livelihood.

8. The Buddha is tall and straight.

The cause for his tall and straight body is merit created from the practice of the abandonment of killing.

9. His elbows and knees do not protrude.

The cause for his elbows and knees not protruding is merit created from the wholehearted practice of positive deeds related to the six perfections.

10. The hairs of his body point upward.

The cause for his body hairs pointing upward is merit created from the practice of helping others to cultivate positive deeds.

11. The ankles are like those of an antelope.

The cause for his ankles being like those of an antelope is merit created from the practice of respectfully giving medicine, artistic knowledge and professional work skill to others.

12. The hands are long and beautiful.

The cause for his long and beautiful hands is merit created from the practice of joyfully giving away anything that others ask for, without ever rejecting them.

13. The male organ is withdrawn.

The cause for his male organ being withdrawn is merit created from the practice of keeping the covenant secret and personal.

14. The body is the color of gold.

The cause for his golden colored body is merit created from the practice of providing a comfortable mat to others for their health and relaxation.

15. The skin is smooth.

The cause for his skin being smooth is merit created through the practice of providing cozy, comfortable and attractive homes to others for their protection from the harmful effects of the elements, like water, heat, cold, wind, etc.

16. Each hair curls to the right.

The cause for each of his hairs curling to the right is merit created from the practice of complete pacification of mental distraction and mental involvement in sensual pleasures.

17. The face is adorned by a coiled hair between his eyebrows.

The cause for his face being adorned with a coiled hair or urna between his eyebrows is merit created from the practice of respectfully treating all beings as one's kind Lama or teacher.

The coiled hair or urna has several characteristics, such as being extremely fine, soft, white and flexible. It becomes as long as forty-five inches when it is pulled and when it is let go, it naturally curls to the right. The tip of the hair is always pointed upward, fragrant and radiating like polished silver.

18. The upper part of the body is like that of a lion.

The cause for his upper body being like that of a lion is merit created from the practice of abandonment of despising others and speaking ironically to others out of pride or vanity.

19. The head and shoulders are perfectly round.

The cause for his head and shoulders being perfectly round is merit created from the practice of living a life that is worthy of the high reverence and praise of others.

20. The shoulders are broad.

The cause for his shoulders being broad is merit created from the practice of providing medicine and medical care to needy ones.

21. He has an excellent sense of taste.

The cause for his excellent sense of taste is merit created from the practice of taking care of sick ones and making healing prayers for them.

22. The body has the proportions of a banyan tree.

The cause for his body having the proportions of a banyan tree is merit created from the practice of taking care of the natural environment, public recreational parks, sacred religious places and forests that are sanctuaries for various kinds of living creatures, and encouraging others to do so as well.

23. There is a protrusion on the crown of the head.

The cause for his crown protrusion is merit created from the practice of giving financial and technical help to build temples, stupas, public prayer halls, etc.

24. The tongue is long.

The cause for his long tongue that can reach up to the hairline and up to the ears is merit created from the practice of speaking gently and always using pleasing words over the three countless eons.

25. The voice is mellifluent.

The cause for his mellifluent voice is merit created from the practice of skillful Dharma teachings spoken in one language but allowing the listeners to understand it in their own language simultaneously.

26. The cheeks are like those of a lion.

The cause for his lion-like cheeks is merit created from the practice of abandonment of idle gossip, false statements, baseless rumors, etc.

27. The teeth are white.

The cause for his teeth being naturally clean and white is merit created from the practice of always being respectful to and praising others rather than blaming or criticizing.

28. There are no gaps between the teeth.

The cause for no gap between his teeth is merit created from the abandonment of five harmful and unwholesome means of livelihood and the cultivation of non harmful and wholesome means of livelihood. The five unwholesome means of livelihood are: flattery, hinting, seeking reward for favor, pretentious behavior and contrived means. The five unwholesome means of livelihood include procuring and selling intoxicating drinks, drugs, meat, poison, weapons, prostitution, and equipment for catching fish, crab, shrimp, lobster, etc. Also considered harmful is controlling others by force of your financial, economic and political power. For example, going to war on the pretext of global and national security, but in fact being motivated by the economic self interest of obtaining oil.

29. The teeth are evenly set.

The cause for his teeth being evenly set is merit created from the practice of speaking truthful words over three countless eons.

30. There are a total of forty teeth.

The cause for having a total of forty teeth is merit created from the practice of never using deceptive words.

31. The eyes are the color of sapphire.

The cause for his eyes being the color of sapphire is merit created from the practice of treating and cherishing all sentient beings without exception as one's only loving child.

32. The eyelashes are like those of a magnificent heifer.

The cause for his eyelashes being like those of a magnificent heifer is merit created from the practice of taking care of all sentient beings without any feeling of attraction, aversion and indifference over the long period of time.

What Are the Eighty Minor Marks of a Buddha?

The eighty minor marks of a Buddha are external marks of physical perfection that are visible for others and from which others can infer the inner distinct and unique spiritual realizations and other enlightened qualities in the Buddha. Each one of the eighty marks of a Buddha has its own unique spiritual and meritorious cause created over the training period in the causal path leading to Buddhahood.

The eighty minor marks are:

1. Buddha's nails are copper colored.

The cause for Buddha's copper colored nails is merit created from the practice of perfection of detachment from all phenomena conditioned by sensory stimulation.

2. His nails are moderately shiny.

The cause for Buddha's nails being moderately shiny is merit created by perfecting the resolution to help all living creatures meet their ultimate spiritual needs.

3. His nails are raised.

The cause for Buddha's nails being raised is merit created from the practice of humility and considering others higher than oneself.

4. His nails are round.

The cause for his nails being round is merit created from the practice of perfection of purification of every single habitual trace left from indulging in actions and behavior that are negative by nature.

5. His nails are broad.

The cause for Buddha's nails being broad is merit created from the practice of perfection of accumulation of virtuous seeds over the long period of training on the causal path leading to Buddhahood.

6. His nails are tapered.

The cause for Buddha's nails being tapered is merit created from the practice of perfection of wisdom realizing selflessness in accordance with the three *yanas* or vehicles. The three yanas or vehicles are:

- *Sravakayana*—hearer vehicle
- *Pratekyabuddhayana*—solitary realizer vehicle
- *Mahayana*—greater vehicle or Bodhisattvayana

The idea of selflessness is equally asserted by the three vehicles as mandatory in order to reach Nirvana or liberation.

7. His veins do not protrude.

The cause for Buddha's veins not protruding is merit created from the practice of abstention from ten negative actions of body, speech and mind, and abstention from five wrong means of livelihood over the long period of time training in the causal path to Enlightenment.

8. His veins are free of knots.

The cause for Buddha's veins being free of knots is merit created from the practice of elimination of all delusional knots in the psyche.

9. His ankles do not protrude.

The cause for Buddha's ankles not protruding is merit created from the practice of wisdom realizing emptiness, which is the subtle and most profound inner nature of all existing phenomena.

10. His feet are even.

The cause for Buddha's feet being even is merit created from the practice of releasing sentient beings from the ocean of Samsara (illusion) that is difficult to cross, and guiding them to the other side, which is Nirvana.

11. He walks with a lion's gait.

The cause for Buddha walking with a lion's gait is merit created from the practice of being so outstanding in appearance that inappropriate thoughts and actions of other people are overwhelmed and suppressed.

12. He walks with an elephant's gait.

The cause for Buddha walking with an elephant's gait is merit created from the practice of being wise and skillful in pacifying harmful and dangerous non-human creatures such as harmful *nagas* (snake demons) and confused spirits.

13. He walks with the gait of a goose.

The cause for Buddha walking with the gait of a goose is merit created from the practice of magical skill in traveling through space to provide timely help to others.

14. He walks with a bull's gait.

The cause for Buddha walking with a bull's gait is merit created from the practice of being wise and skillful in leading and guiding sentient beings in the realm of cyclic existence.

15. His gait tends to the right.

The cause for Buddha's gait tending to the right is merit created from the mindful spiritual practice of clockwise circumambulation.

16. His gait is elegant.

The cause for Buddha's gait being elegant is merit created from the practice of moving in a way that is pleasing and soothing to others.

17. His gait is steady.

The cause for Buddha's gait being steady is merit created from the practice of mindfulness in being truthful and honest at all times and to all others.

18. His body is well covered.

The cause for Buddha's body being well covered is merit created from the practice of always admiring and praising others' good qualities and wholesome deeds.

19. His body looks as if it were polished.

The cause for Buddha's body looking as if were polished is merit created from the practice of thoroughly freeing body, speech and mind from the trace of delusions and obstructions.

20. His body is well proportioned.

The cause for Buddha's body being well proportioned is merit created from the practice of perfection of giving teachings in accordance to the disciple's mental capability, inclination and predisposition.

21. His body is clean and pure.

The cause for Buddha's body being clean and pure is merit created from the practice of wholesome activities of body, speech and mind with no possibility that unwholesome activities can manifest.

22. His body is smooth.

The cause for Buddha's body being naturally smooth is merit created from the practice of unconditional great compassion that cherishes all living creatures at all times, under any circumstances, never giving a thought to abandoning them.

23. His body is perfect.

The cause for Buddha's body being perfect is merit created from the practice of the perfection of permanently freeing his mind from delusional and karmic stains.

24. His sex organs are fully developed.

The cause for Buddha's sex organs being fully developed is merit created from the practice of perfecting the ethical discipline to overcome all sorts of distorted thoughts and emotions that serve as an immediate cause for the arising of negative actions of body and speech.

25. His physical bearing is excellent and dignified.

The cause for Buddha's physical bearing being excellent and dignified is merit created from the practice of giving useful and appealing teachings that fulfill the immediate needs of listeners.

26. His steps are even.

The cause for Buddha's steps being perfectly even is merit created from the practice of unbiased and equal attitudes towards all sentient beings without any sense of discrimination or favoritism.

27. His eyes are perfect.

The cause for Buddha's eyes being perfectly fresh and undistracted is merit created from the practice of giving teachings that naturally generate positive qualities in the mindstreams of listeners.

28. He is youthful.

The cause for Buddha always being youthful is merit created from the practice of the skilled demonstration of various analogies and examples, thus making the teaching easy to understand by the listeners.

29. His body is not sunken.

The cause for Buddha's body being not sunken is merit created from the practice of not feeling discouraged, disheartened and depressed due to meeting with hardship and difficulties.

30. His body is broad.

The cause for Buddha's body being broad is merit created from the practice of perfecting the root of virtue in a unique, sublime and superior manner.

31. His body is not loose.

The cause for Buddha's body not being loose is merit created from the practice of the total eradication of karmic seeds that makes uncontrolled samsaric birth inevitable.

32. His limbs are well proportioned.

The cause for Buddha's limbs being well proportioned is merit created from the practice of giving teachings on the interdependent co-arising twelve links, in their causal sequential order, as well as in their reversed order, in the effort to liberate sentient beings from samsaric existence.

33. His vision is clear and unblurred.

The cause for Buddha's vision being clear and unblurred is merit created from the practice of making sure to convey the various means and ways to obtain higher fortunate rebirth and the definite attainment of Nirvana and Buddhahood.

34. His belly is round.

The cause for Buddha's belly being round is merit created from the practice of skillful means of teaching on the vastness and varieties of paths and methods.

35. His belly is perfectly moderate.

The cause for Buddha's belly being perfectly moderate is merit created from the practice of eliminating every single trace and stain of samsaric flaws, thereby eliminating the possibility of ever being affected by those stains again.

36. His belly is not long.

The cause for Buddha's belly not being long is merit created from the practice of eliminating egotistic pride.

37. His belly doesn't bulge.

The cause for the Buddha's belly not bulging is merit created from the practice of applying antidotal wisdom for the eradication of every single trace of samsaric faults and stains.

38. His navel is deep.

The cause of Buddha's navel being deep is merit created from the realization of the profound and subtle mode in which phenomena actually exist in reality.

39. His navel winds to the right.

The cause of the Buddha's navel winding to the right is merit created from the practice of giving spiritual instruction in accordance with a disciple's immediate needs and spiritual capability.

40. He is perfectly handsome.

The cause for the perfect handsomeness of Buddha's body is merit created from the practice of helping others to cultivate appealing behaviors and conduct in their body, speech and thought patterns.

41. His habits are clean.

The cause for Buddha's habits being clean is merit created from the practice of purifying his mind from the stains of delusion, thereby being mentally undefiled under all conditions.

42. His body is free of moles and discoloration.

The cause of Buddha's body being free of moles and discoloration is merit created from the practice of not teaching Dharma topics or practices to students who have not yet developed the spiritual maturity to understand them.

43. His hands are soft as cotton wool.

The cause of Buddha's hands being soft as cotton wool is merit created from the practice of generously giving teachings on the cultivation of inner causes and conditions to obtain an attractive physical body with a naturally calm and peaceful mental state.

44. The lines of his palms are clear.

The cause for the lines of Buddha's palms being clear is merit created from the practice of treating all sentient beings as one would treat loved ones and close friends.

45. The lines of his palms are deep.

The cause for the lines of Buddha's palms being deep is merit created from the practice of perfecting the realization of the true nature of all phenomena.

46. The lines of Buddha's palms are long.

The cause for the lines of Buddha's palms being long is merit created from the practice of benefiting others for their temporary and ultimate needs, and giving flawless spiritual guidance in accordance to their mental predisposition.

47. His face is not overly long.

The cause for Buddha's face being not overly long is merit created from the practice of giving various instructions in accordance with the different levels of spiritual maturity on the part of disciples.

48. His lips are red like copper.

The cause for Buddha's lips being red like copper is merit created from the practice of realizing all existing phenomena being empty of intrinsic existence.

49. His tongue is pliant.

The cause for Buddha's tongue being extremely pliant is merit created from the practice of disciplining his disciples with pleasant and soothing words.

50. His tongue is thin.

The cause for Buddha's extremely thin tongue is merit created from the practice of giving teachings by presenting various types of valid logical reasons and avenues for validating the truth of teaching materials. Nothing taught should be accepted out of blind faith and mere respect for the teacher.

51. His tongue is red.

The cause for Buddha's tongue being perfectly red is merit created from the practice of showing correct ethical conduct to tame the body, speech and mind of those who are obsessed with grasping at "I" and "mine" with a strong sense of attachment.

52. His voice is like thunder.

The cause for Buddha's voice being like thunder is merit created from the practice of not concealing personal flaws and wrongdoings, and living a life free of fear of others finding out one's wrongdoings, flaws and imperfections, etc.

53. His voice is sweet and gentle.

The cause for Buddha's voice being sweet and gentle is merit created from the practice of consistently using appealing words to open others' hearts and minds towards Dharma and to a wholesome way of life.

54. His teeth are round.

The cause for Buddha's teeth being perfectly round is merit created from the practice of cessation of the nine ever-binding factors in samsaric existence.

These nine factors that bind us to samsaric existence are:

~ Attachment
~ Anger

- Egotistic pride
- Confusion
- Denying the facts of reality
- Maintaining the superiority of oneself
- Deluded doubt
- Jealousy
- Miserliness

Each one of the ever binding factors contains an element of clinging and grasping onto cyclic existence that is by nature subject to impermanence, decay, sickness, aging and much unexpected pain and suffering.

55. His teeth are sharp.

The cause for Buddha's teeth being sharp is merit created from the practice of releasing sentient beings from Samsara, even those who are extremely difficult to release due to the density of their delusions.

56. His teeth are white.

The cause for Buddha's teeth being naturally white is merit created from the practice of giving teachings on pure ethics that naturally give birth to every virtue.

57. His teeth are even.

The cause for Buddha's teeth being perfectly even is merit created from the practice of abiding in the realization of the oneness of Samsara and Nirvana within the reality of one's mind.

58. His teeth are tapered.

The cause for Buddha's teeth being tapered is merit created from the practice of skillfully showing the three yanas or paths to be cultivated in an orderly sequence.

59. His nose is prominent.

The cause for Buddha's nose being prominent is merit created from the practice of perfection of skillful means and the capability to live with a wisdom realizing emptiness as the supreme enlightened quality.

60. His nose is naturally clean.

The cause for Buddha's nose being naturally clean is merit created from the practice of keeping promises, and being honest, truthful and trustworthy for all spiritual trainees.

61. His eyes are clear and wide.

The cause for Buddha's eyes being clear and wide is merit created from the practice of giving elaborate and vast Mahayana teachings on the various skills required to fulfill sentient beings' temporary worldly needs and their ultimate spiritual attainment.

62. His eyelashes are thick.

The cause for Buddha's eyelashes being thick is merit created from the practice of liberating limitless sentient beings from the ocean of Samsara.

63. The black and white parts of his eyes are well defined and are like lotus petals.

The cause for the black and white parts of Buddha's eyes being well defined and like lotus petals is merit created from the practice of benefiting and satisfying even those who are extremely difficult to please and satisfy.

64. His eyebrows are long.

The cause for Buddha's eyebrows being long is merit created from the practice of gaining psychic power to see upcoming events and acting in accordance with that insight.

65. His eyebrows are smooth.

The cause for Buddha's eyebrows being smooth is merit created from the practice of being wise and skillful in training others through a peaceful path rather than a harsh and extreme path of self-mortification.

66. His eyebrows are soft and shiny.

The cause for Buddha's eyebrows being soft and shiny is merit created from the cultivation of being mentally saturated by virtuous feelings and wholesomeness.

67. His eyebrows are evenly hairy.

The cause for Buddha's eyebrows being evenly hairy is merit created from the practice of always seeing the disadvantages and negativities of afflictive thoughts and emotions without feeling the slightest sense of positive qualities in them.

68. His hands are long and extended.

The cause for Buddha's hands being long and extended is merit created from the practice of working on helping sentient beings to eliminate their samsaric seed in general and, particularly, to eliminate the karmic seed for unfortunate rebirth in the lower realms of existence.

69. His ears are of equal size.

The cause for Buddha's ears being of equal size is merit created from the practice of overcoming attachment to existence. This type of attachment is most difficult to overcome.

70. His hearing is perfect.

The cause for Buddha's hearing being perfect is merit created from the practice of bringing sentient beings' minds into the state of happiness, joy, serenity and tranquility.

71. His forehead is well formed.

The cause for Buddha's forehead being well formed is merit created from the practice of making his mind unwavering and undistracted by the force of sixty-two types of wrong views and the extreme views of nihilism and absolutism.

72. His forehead is broad.

The cause for Buddha's forehead being broad is merit created from the practice of defeating all negative forces, false accusations, defamations and insults directed towards someone else.

73. His head is very large.

The cause for Buddha's head being very large is merit created from the practice of perfection of aspirational prayers and wishes to attain Enlightenment in order to be of ultimate service to all sentient beings.

74. His hair is as black as a bumblebee.

The cause for Buddha's hair being as black as a bumblebee is merit created from the practice of total eradication of desirous attachment to the external sensual world of form, sound, smell, taste and touch.

75. His hair is thick.

The cause for Buddha's hair being thick is merit created from the practice of the meditative antidote that eliminates obstructions that need to be eradicated on reaching the Path of Seeing and the Path of Meditation (two of the five paths to Buddhahood), as well as eliminating the latent seeds that are the primary source of delusion.

76. His hair is soft.

The cause for Buddha's soft hair is merit from the practice of being compassionate, skillful and gentle in bringing others to Dharma.

77. His hair is untangled.

The cause for Buddha's hair being untangled is merit created from the practice of not allowing his mind to be disturbed by the force of distorted emotions of attachment, aversion, jealousy, fear, sadness and confusion.

78. His hair is not unruly.

The cause for Buddha's hair not being unruly is merit created from the practice of totally eliminating harsh, insulting, humiliating and other displeasing words and speeches and consistently using pleasing, sweet, gentle and respectful words and speeches towards others.

79. His hair is fragrant.

The cause for Buddha's hair being fragrant is merit created from the practice of sincerely and respectfully making many material offerings such as fragrant flowers to the enlightened beings and dedicating the merit to the cause of Enlightenment.

80. His hands and feet are marked with auspicious emblems.

The cause for Buddha's feet being marked with auspicious emblems is merit created from the practice of strong and unshakable spiritual motivation to work on internal spiritual causes for Enlightenment, and to make living creatures happy, with attractive physical emblems expressing inner joy and perfection.

    The above eighty minor physical marks of Buddha are explicit expressions of the existence of various inner spiritual realizations in the Buddha. Buddha's followers, as well as non followers, can infer the existence of unique spiritual realizations in the Buddha by merely seeing the physical marks of the Buddha.
    Buddha's impressive and attractive physical marks are present for the sole purpose of inspiring his followers to walk along the peaceful path shown by him.

What Is Svabhavakaya?

Svabhavakaya is a Sanskrit word meaning the natural truth body. The natural truth body is not a physical or material body. It is a factor of cleanliness from adventitious stains of mind and lack of mind's inherent existence.

There are two types of natural truth body. One is the factor of purity from adventitious stains of mind. It is called the natural truth body of cessation within the Buddha's mental continuum. In Sanskrit it is called *agantuvisuddhibhagibuta-Svabhavakaya*. The other type of natural truth body is a factor of the intrinsically pure nature of Buddha's mental continuum. In Sanskrit it is called *svabhavavisuddhibhuta-Svabhavakaya*, which means intrinsically pure nature body.

In brief, the emptiness of the Buddha's mental continuum is called intrinsically pure nature body of the Buddha. The natural truth body of the Buddha is a natural effect of perfection of the eradication of adventitious stains of the mind and of the mistaken notion of self.

What Is Jnanadharmakaya?

Jnanadharmakaya is a Sanskrit word meaning wisdom truth body. Again, this is not a physical or material body. It is the highest form of wisdom which simultaneously realizes the ultimate reality of the emptiness of all phenomena while retaining the full ascertainment of the relative and deceptive appearance of conventional reality that has temporary conventional fulfilling meaning in it.

However, emptiness is not realized by the wisdom truth body simultaneously with the realization of the relative reality of deceptive appearance, and the relative reality of deceptive appearance is not realized simultaneously with the realization of emptiness. Therefore, there are two types of wisdom truth body. They are:

1. The wisdom truth body realizing the relative reality of the deceptive appearance that has temporary conventional fulfilling meaning in it.
2. The wisdom truth body realizing the ultimate reality of emptiness of all phenomena without the interference of any sense of intrinsic-ness.

The wisdom truth body of the Buddha is the final effect of the perfection of actualization of pure wisdom consciousness.

About the Author

Geshe-la obviously has all the Buddhist knowledge and personal experience, and he reflects that with his calmness but also with an incredible sense of humor. He uses his amazing vocabulary to express complex concepts according to everyone's individual mental activity. ~ Charleston Magazine

GESHE DAKPA TOPGYAL, A Tibetan Buddhist monk, was born in the Western region of Tibet, and fled to India at the age of six with his family due to the Chinese invasion of Tibet. He entered Drepung Loseling Monastery at the age of ten and received his Geshe degree (Doctorate of Religion and Philosophy) twenty-two years later in 1992.

Before coming to the United States, he taught in Europe for a number of years. Between 1993 and 1994, he visited one hundred and twenty American cities giving lectures on Tibetan Buddhism and culture, and led a number of meditation retreats. Currently, he teaches students year round and serves as spiritual director of the Charleston Tibetan Society Dharma Center as well as the South Carolina Dharma Group in Columbia, South Carolina. In addition to the book list in this text, Geshe Topgyal has published numerous practice manuals.

www.ingramcontent.com/pod-product-compliance
Lightning Source LLC
Chambersburg PA
CBHW030152100526
44592CB00009B/233